A JOURNEY OF HONESTY

A JOURNEY OF HONESTY

An Extraordinary Account of the
Life of **Prof. E. Balagurusamy**

Geetha Nair *and* **Paa Krishnan**
with inputs from **Dr Bindu Vijayakumar**

RUPA

Published by
Rupa Publications India Pvt. Ltd 2023
7/16, Ansari Road, Daryaganj
New Delhi 110002

Sales Centres:
Bengaluru Chennai
Hyderabad Jaipur Kathmandu
Kolkata Mumbai Prayagraj

Copyright © EBG Foundation 2023
Photos courtesy: EBG Foundation
Illustrations: B. Senthil Kumar (Pillai)

Copyright of the photographs vests with the respective photographer/copyright owner. While every effort has been made to trace copyright holders and obtain permission, this has not been possible in all cases; any omissions brought to our attention will be remedied in future editions.

The views and opinions expressed in this book are the authors' own and the facts are as reported by them, which have been verified to the extent possible, and the publishers are not in any way liable for the same.

All rights reserved.
No part of this publication may be reproduced, transmitted or stored in a retrieval system, in any form or by any means, electronic, mechanical, photocopying, recording or otherwise, without the prior permission of the publisher.

P-ISBN: 978-93-5702-178-4
E-ISBN: 978-93-5702-170-8

First impression 2023

10 9 8 7 6 5 4 2 3 1

The moral right of the authors has been asserted.

Printed in India

This book is sold subject to the condition that it shall not, by way of trade or otherwise, be lent, resold, hired out or otherwise circulated, without the publisher's prior consent, in any form of binding or cover other than that in which it is published.

Contents

Foreword by R. Chandrashekhar — vii
Foreword by Justice P. Sathasivam — ix
Foreword by Dr M.S. Swaminathan — xi

1. Warm…Compassionate…Energetic — 1
2. Goats Pave the Way — 6
3. The Verandah School — 10
4. Street Light to Limelight — 16
5. On the Wings of Science — 23
6. Forever Optimistic — 27
7. Hard Work Pays — 30
8. Anti-Hindi Agitation — 37
9. In Love with Electricity — 42
10. A New World to Conquer — 51
11. Self-confidence — 54
12. Aiming for the Sky — 61
13. 'I Stick to My Rights' — 66
14. A Strong Sense of Direction — 71
15. New Avenues — 77
16. Spring Comes — 81
17. Fragrance for the Flower — 85
18. Good Tidings in the Path of Life — 90
19. Andhra Pradesh Beckons — 97
20. Viral Attack on Democracy — 103
21. PSG Invites EBG — 111

22. Dedicated to the Core	116
23. A New Enterprise in Bangalore	123
24. Challenges and Achievements	128
25. The Lion Roars at Anna University	135
26. The Dauntless Vice-Chancellor	144
27. Courage and Compassion	158
28. Strong Determination	163
29. Decisions that Change Fortunes	170
30. Synonymous with Efficiency	178
31. Standing Tall Before the Law	185
32. The Tree Thanks the One Who Sowed the Seed	191
33. Delhi Calls Again	196
34. Painful Parting	207
35. Uncompromising Stand	211
36. Humane to the Core	217
37. Abdul Kalam's Brother?	227
EBG: An Illustrious Life	232
Acknowledgements	235

Foreword

Higher education in India suffers from many drawbacks. Most people sit back and lament that the 'system' is failing us. This biography of Dr E. Balagurusamy is a clear message that motivated, idealistic individuals are crucial for nation-building and make all the difference. It is a reinforcement of Mahatma Gandhi's wise words: 'Be the change you wish to see'.

Throughout his career as an academic, educator and scientific and technological author, Dr E. Balagurusamy held important academic positions like the Vice-Chancellor of Anna University as well as positions with a broader ambit, such as a member of the Union Public Service Commission (UPSC). In these positions, he influenced a whole generation of young Indians, directly and indirectly. His principled, morally upright and transparent approach to all issues as well as people imbued the younger generation with the same ideals. In an era where pragmatism often trumps principles, the importance of such a contribution to the nation cannot be overemphasized.

This biography brings forth the many remarkable facets and virtues of a wonderful man. Even better, the book uncovers this, not by elaborate prose, but through a phenomenally large array of real-life episodes from Dr E. Balagurusamy's life in brief vignettes that beautifully capture the underlying virtues of the man. The exceptional mix of the highest degree of professional drive, competence and depth of knowledge, combined with the aspects of empathy, compassion and humility are the hallmarks of this extraordinary individual.

These virtues, while admirable, are perhaps easier to bring into play when circumstances are conducive. But what makes his contribution stand out is his relentless and uncompromising response even in the face of crippling constraints. Clearly, his was a life lived on his own terms, whatever the position or circumstances. This biography reveals an elevating truth; it is possible to be highly principled and yet reach the highest positions in the present-day environment in the country.

That, in itself, is a truly inspiring message conveyed through this biography to all people—young and old. It is a captivating book that can be enjoyed at many levels, especially its real-life episodes, short anecdotes and examples of how values and principles can and must be preserved in the face of sometimes overwhelming adversity, and the need for a soft, compassionate human touch, in the absence of which even high principles have a grating quality that robs them of their lustre.

I have known EBG since his days at Hyderabad in the eighties and have had the occasion to interact with him on and off thereafter. I knew him as an academic and as a warm, friendly person and was well aware of his many qualities. Nevertheless, this biography was a revelation to me in many respects.

I am sure readers will enjoy the book and it will serve as an inspiration for generations to come.

—R. Chandrashekhar
Chairman, Centre for The Digital Future
Former Secretary, IT & Telecom, Government of India
Ex-President, NASSCOM

Foreword

Dr E. Balagurusamy has been known to me since he was the vice-chancellor of Anna University. I was then serving as a judge of the Madras High Court, way back in 2002. I am aware of all his strenuous efforts, fighting to raise the standard of the university, for which he also faced several litigations.

I am happy to read his biography. Dr Balagurusamy is an ace academician, scientist and above all, a philanthropist. His life may prove to be a model for the younger generation to follow.

Dr Balagurusamy and I served as vice-chancellor and High Court Judge, respectively. Similarly, our journey continued during our services in New Delhi as he was a member of the Union Public Service Commission (UPSC) when I happened to hold judicial office in the Supreme Court. As contemporaries in the capital city, we felt close to each other, as we are both from Tamil Nadu. His innovative and creative skills in handling the selection of civil service officers and their disciplinary cases are commendable.

In addition to this, it must be recalled that we both are from ordinary agricultural families in remote hamlets of Tamil Nadu. Above all, both of us are from neighbouring districts, where we now live as well. So, as a person from such a background, I can empathize with the struggles and challenges Dr Balagurusamy might have faced in achieving heights as a world-renowned educationist, author and scientist.

The biography of Dr Balagurusamy, *A Journey of Honesty*, contains several anecdotes that are significant. But I can say that this book is not just a compilation of tales; every chapter carries a message that will motivate youth and teachers in their careers and lives to strive for more remarkable achievements. It is interesting to note that the authors have placed suitable couplets of the *Thirukkural*, written by the saint poet Thiruvalluvar, at the beginning of every chapter, which enhances this biography's standard. Every couplet has a message relating to the life of Dr Balagurusamy and how he was able to succeed.

One can read books written for entertainment only once. Educational books are meant to be read a few times to gain knowledge. But this biography crosses these limitations as it is written for motivation. I reiterate that the biography of Dr Balagurusamy will create an impact on those who read it.

I pray to the Almighty to bless Dr E. Balagurusamy to live long, hale and healthy and serve the educational field and society for many more years.

—**Justice P. Sathasivam**
Former Chief Justice of India and former Governor of Kerala

Foreword

I was delighted to read the biography of my long-time friend, Dr E. Balagurusamy. I have known him through the various visits he made to our foundation to discuss various crucial matters.

If we say farmers are the backbone of India, we can also say that scientists are the face of India. Dr Balagurusamy stands at the top of the list of such scientists. He firmly believes that the country's growth can be taken forward only when scientists and technologists are shaped to suit future generations.

Dr Balagurusamy is a strong proponent of sustainable development, which includes social, economic and environment developments. He banned the use of plastic and artificial drinks on the Anna University campus during his tenure as vice-chancellor.

His principle of life is not living for himself but living for others. He always cared for the welfare of students and was keen on improving the standards of education and educational institutions. His contributions to making students more creative, innovative and productive through various schemes in the university are remarkable.

Dr Balagurusamy is a very good administrator and a person of integrity. It is rare to find such a person: born in a farmer's family in a small hamlet to go on to hold the highest academic offices.

His biography cites several instances of how determined he was to study despite many hurdles. He used to cycle for over ten kilometres to reach his school on time. Impressed by his performance, the headmaster of the secondary school where he studied remarked, 'Holds the first rank in school, deserves encouragement.' This is exceptional. Perhaps the headmaster thought that the future crop was known in the germ.

The struggles to continue his higher education, complete research work and take up teaching assignments will likely motivate those who are themselves in such phases of their life. His perseverance, determination, self-confidence, hard work, honesty and dedication will show them that these are the means towards success.

Similar to his remarkable services as vice-chancellor of Anna University, Dr Balagurusamy forged a record as a member of the UPSC by introducing innovative methods of selecting candidates for the Indian Administrative Service (IAS). The talent and honesty he had shown throughout his professional deeds are remarkable. Dr Balagurusamy had the guts to reject many lucrative offers that went against his principles.

This is not a book with a chronology of some events; rather, it will prove to be an inspiration to the younger generation on how purity and honesty can lead to success in life.

The style of the authors who placed an appropriate *Thirukkural* couplet with its meaning at the beginning of every chapter is laudable.

—Dr M.S. Swaminathan
Founder Chairman, M.S. Swaminathan Research Foundation,
Chennai,
Former Member of Parliament (Rajya Sabha)

1
Warm...Compassionate...Energetic

*What does a man from wisdom gain,
if he pines not at other's pain?*[*]

—Thirukkural 315

The authorities were taken aback when they heard that 'HE' had arrived at their college that very morning! No college management would expect that the vice-chancellor of their governing university would personally visit the college for such an issue. Upon arriving at the scene, the vice-chancellor called three students who were standing in front of the college. He started interacting with these boys who appeared timid. All three of them came from impoverished families.

After this, the vice-chancellor entered the college principal's room and asked the authorities seated there why the boys had been made to stand outside. Even in their wildest dreams the college authorities had never imagined that the vice-chancellor would question them openly and issue a strict warning.

'Come on...tell me, why do you harass these students? Who gave you the authority to ill-treat them like this?' he thundered.

Under the fire of such stern words from Dr E. Balagurusamy, the vice-chancellor of Anna University, Chennai, the authorities were tongue-tied and could only stand benumbed.

---

[*]All couplets, except four of them, have been translated by Yogi Suddhanand Bharati.

WHAT HAD HAPPENED?

The three students, who had gained admission to this private engineering college at Thiruvallur, 40 kilometres from Chennai, were not permitted by the college authorities to attend their classes. Unfortunately, the three students had not clearly understood the cause of this discrimination and punishment. They stood waiting at the gate every day, from morning till evening, hoping that they would be allowed to enter the college and attend their classes.

The reason given by the college authorities for the punishment was strange. No criminal charges had been issued against the three students. They had not indulged in any vandalism or damaged college property. They had not been involved in any illegal activity. They had not misbehaved on the college campus. Nothing of this sort had happened. The only 'crime' they had committed was that they had been born into low-income families!

The three students were worried. Many days had passed since their classes had started. When would their problem be solved? What would be their future? Whom could they approach for help?

LIKE LORD KRISHNA

'Call me in times of need, and I will appear before you.' This is what Lord Krishna has promised in the Bhagavad Gita. But here, the needy did not have to call; Dr Balagurusamy, the vice-chancellor of Anna University, came to their help without waiting for a request from these poor, aggrieved students. The matter was brought to his notice only a few days after it had begun. But as soon as he knew about it, he personally came to the college. First, he talked with the students who were waiting outside the portals of the college.

'What is the problem, my boys? Tell me, don't hesitate,' he asked them.

'Sir, we are poor, but we paid the college fees when we were admitted here. That amount was earned with great difficulty. But now the authorities insist that we have to pay fifteen thousand rupees more as bus fees. They will allow us to attend classes only after we pay that amount. We don't have the money for that. Our parents somehow managed to pay the tuition fees. The government has a scheme subsidising bus fares for students. But to avail that, we need a certificate from the college saying that we arestudents of this institution. The college authorities refuse to issue that certificate.'

The boys could hardly speak through their tears. Their fathers were ordinary workers; one was a watchman, the other a coolie and the third was an agricultural labourer.

Dr Balagurusamy felt his own throat constrict in pain upon hearing the boys' words. Now that he had gathered all the information he had wanted from the victims themselves, he turned to the principal and the other authorities of the college.

In a voice brimming with rage, he asked, 'Why do you trouble these boys like this? Haven't they paid the college fees? Then why do you harass them for bus fees? That is not compulsory. If they cannot pay for the college bus, let them use public transport or ride cycles to come to their classes. How can you make students stand outside the college gate because they haven't fulfilled your demand?'

The principal and the others had nothing to say. They were sweating, afraid of the consequences.

Dr Balagurusamy continued, 'I used to go to school on my cycle. If anyone had made a similar demand of me, I would have been forced to discontinue my studies. Don't you know what a college is for? Your duty is to teach the students and make arrangements and facilities for them to learn. All these buildings may belong to the management of the college, but it is the university that decides what subjects are to be taught here, and the university also conducts the examinations. Those who join this college are the students of Anna University. They will get the degree from Anna University once they have completed their course successfully. No one has the authority to stop them from studying here. Don't you have a conscience? How would you feel if your children were forced to stand outside their colleges in the hot sun like this? Did you think of the parents who have sent these boys to your college? Can't you imagine the pain and humiliation that they have gone through? Let those who want to travel by the college bus do so, but why should you insist on everyone paying for it? You have to teach them well. See that you do that properly. If the University takes

Prof. Balagurusamy advising college administrators.

a decision, this college can be closed down now, this very minute. Do you understand?'

Nothing more needed to be said to make the college authorities toe the line. The principal gave instructions to allow the boys to attend their classes. As Dr Balagurusamy left the place, the three boys said nothing. They only stood with folded hands, as if in front of the Almighty. This was the first time—maybe the only incident in the history of Tamil Nadu and the whole of India—that a vice-chancellor intervened *directly* when justice had been denied to students.

As Dr Balagurusamy, the vice-chancellor, returned from the engineering college, scenes from his childhood flashed through his mind. His childhood and adolescence had been one of deprivation. Even when he had started his education, limited facilities in the village of his youth had made his life very difficult back then. Still, he had overcome his adverse circumstances and begun a career.

As soon as he reached his office at the university, he issued a circular to all the colleges, prohibiting the college authorities from collecting bus fees compulsorily. At that time, it was an important, path-breaking order issued by a university.

2
Goats Pave the Way

Wisdom checks the straying senses,
expels evils, impels goodness.

—Thirukkural 422

'Ah! Rain... It's raining...! It's raining!'
The little boy tending to the goats jumped about in joy as the rain drenched him.

The sun had been scorching, and the boy ran around in the unexpected shower, enjoying himself. Which little boy would not frolic in the rain! This boy lived in the village, tended to the goats and grew close to nature. In the excitement of the moment, the little boy forgot about his goats; he was far too busy playing around as if he were one of the lambs under his care.

Suddenly, he heard people shouting and running towards him. 'Your goats! They have fallen from the terrace...they have been killed.'

The boy stood still in shock. Darkness seemed to envelop him. In a daze, he ran towards the old building. There, in a deep pit, he saw two of his biggest goats lying dead, covered in their own blood. It was a heartbreaking sight for the little boy. He started crying out loud. A tragedy was unfolding before him. This would change the course of his life...

This was what fate had in store for him!

None who passed that way, travelling from Aravakurichi, in Karur district of Tamil Nadu, going down the Rangamalai on to Dindigul, would fail to notice the beauty of the village the boy lived in. The paddy fields spread a green carpet over the land, welcoming the visitor's eyes to rest on its serenity.

This boy was a member of a family of farmers who toiled in its fields. Today, that small path is no longer there. In its place runs National Highway 7—connecting Salem and Madurai—a part of the network of highways running from Srinagar to Kanyakumari. It is the longest highway in the country.

Several years ago, the village of Andipattikottai, ten kilometres away from Aravakurichi, would not merit even a pin-prick on a map. The people in that village did not get the news when India gained independence on 15 August 1947. Modern means of communication had not touched the hamlet. The other villages around were no different in any respect. Like the other boys in the village of Andipattikottai, this boy too engaged himself in looking after the goats and doing odd work in the fields. During the rainy season, the dark clouds would cover the sun by five in the evening. It was a good place to raise goats. The boy had two nanny goats and four little kids.

Green grass grew abundantly on the floors of the old, abandoned building. The goats had been on the terrace, enjoying the crop of grass when it started to rain. Forgetting everything else the boy had run out of the building to dance in the rain. The little goats were standing on the narrow sunshade. The mother goats, while trying to get to the kids, slipped and fell. Their bones were crushed; the two older nanny goats suffered a painful death.

The boy did not think of the punishment that awaited him from his father for his negligence. He was more concerned about the four kids who had lost their mothers.

That was the end of his life as a shepherd.

He started working in the field. Plucking weeds was the first work assigned to him. Even as he went on with his work in silence, the tragedy that had befallen his goats never left his mind. He could never remain unaffected by the sufferings of others. Still, isn't it said that time will erase all pains?

People around him noticed how he concentrated on his work; he did not pay heed to anyone while working. Later, as they saw him rise to greater heights in life, they would think about the saying that the strength of the crop can be seen in the first bud.

The boy had the strength of mind to be unmindful about small

The tragic incident that killed a few goats left E. Balagurusamy heart-broken

things; instead, his mind was full of kindness for the downtrodden—these were qualities that took him to the heights of glory. This boy, who started his life plucking weeds from the field, grew up to become the famous 'Professor Balagurusamy', an eminent educationist and an untiring fighter against all social inequalities. With the same earnestness with which he had removed the unwanted weeds from the field, he took a firm stand against all evil in the field of education. He was responsible for many of the reforms and new concepts in the arena of education in Tamil Nadu and he left the field in a much better state when he retired as the vice-chancellor of Anna University.

3

The Verandah School

Like poor before rich they yearn
For knowledge: the low never learn.

—Thirukkural 395

Perumal, the village teacher, spoke to the seven-year-old Balagurusamy as he was working in the field, 'You stop working in the field and come to my school. I will teach you.'

'I don't want to study. I am happy with what I am doing. I won't come,' came the immediate reply. Balagurusamy was not attracted by the offer the schoolmaster had made. The boy knew that his father was particularly affectionate towards him for he believed that his son's hands were especially blessed. If the boy plucked the weeds, the crop planted there would provide a very good yield.

In those days, government schools were not common in villages. There were a few private establishments where a teacher sat on the verandah of a house and taught the children. Such a private school, known as 'verandah' school, had started functioning in Balagurusamy's village that year and Perumal, who had offered to teach him, was the master in charge of that school. Children from the age of five to fifteen were all enrolled in his class. There was no division into different classes; all the students were in the same class and there was only one teacher. The master would teach them all arithmetic, science, history and Tamil.

Since childhood, Balagurusamy was adamant about doing what he considered right. So he was not ready to change his mind about attending Perumal's classes.

'No, I won't come. I don't want to study.' He had made his stance quite clear.

However, the master lifted him up physically and started to take him to the school. But the resisting boy jumped and ran away.

'This is the nature of all boys. They will show some obstinacy at first. That will change gradually. The elders should understand this and act accordingly,' said Perumal to Ellappa Naicker, Balagurusamy's father, when he met him. Somehow, whether by the grace of the Goddess of Learning or under the persuasion of the schoolmaster, Balagurusamy, who had decided to spend the rest of his life on the farm, agreed to join the school.

There might have been another reason for Balagurusamy's change of heart. The pain that assailed him on seeing his goat lying dead in the pit had continued to haunt him. The boy felt that a change of atmosphere, from the fields to the school, would help him forget that incident.

Once he had joined the school, Balagurusamy excelled in everything that was taught there. The schoolmaster was surprised to see such understanding and talent in the boy. The boy also found in himself a passionate fervour to master all that he could. Soon, Balagurusamy was the only student who could answer any questions that the teacher asked in arithmetic. The same was true of all other subjects. He attended his classes regularly and concentrated on what was being taught in them. He seemed to be driven and gave all his attention to whatever he was doing. This ability stayed with him throughout his career, making him work tirelessly, sometimes without taking leave even for a single day. He was never found wanting in any respect, even as he went on to hold very demanding posts. Sincerity and dedication were his hallmarks throughout.

In the village, once a child had attended the private verandah school for five years, he could join the sixth standard in any regular school nearby. But Balagurusamy completed his education in all the subjects in two and a half years. He topped all the tests and in all the subjects. Perumal was delighted to see the boy develop into a dedicated student after being so adamant that he did not want to study.

Thus, by March 1955, Balagurusamy was ready to join the bigger, regular government school. But no such school was available nearby at that time.

Thiru K. Kamaraj had taken charge as the chief minister of Tamil Nadu, back in April 1954. He gave the utmost importance to the development of education in his state. He started elementary schools in all the villages of Tamil Nadu, which then replaced the private verandah schools. An elementary school was started in the village of Andipattikottai and the people were happy and relieved when the government took over the responsibility of providing education to the children.

Balagurusamy later recalled the greatness of Thiru Kamaraj. 'If Thiru Kamaraj had not come into power at that time, how would a poor boy like me have got the chance to forge ahead in life through education? Will we ever see a great leader like him again?' Balagurusamy has repeated these words often when he addressed public gatherings.

When Balagurusamy applied for admission in the new elementary school, the master insisted that he had to be in the fifth standard. Though the schoolmaster realized that the boy was brilliant, he also knew that Balagurusamy had been in the private school only for two and a half years. Moreover, the elementary school could accommodate only students from first to fifth standard.

But Balagurusamy was vexed. Why should he attend the fifth standard again when he had studied all the portions already? Balagurusamy was not ready to accept the master's decision and therefore he refused to join the school.

His father, Ellappa Naicker, was saddened to think that his son would again have to work in the fields in the scorching heat of the sun. His elder son was already working in the field. He did not want Balagurusamy also to have the same fate. So the father made Balagurusamy work in a grocery store in the village run by a man called Muthusamy. Though disappointed at being denied a chance to continue his education, Balagurusamy obeyed his father and went to work in the shop.

There was another reason that prompted Ellappa Naicker to send his son to the shop to work. He had observed that just as the crop planted by Balagurusamy yielded a bounteous harvest, money also seemed to multiply in the boy's hands. The parents used to refer proudly to Balagurusamy as their 'lucky son'. He could make calculations with great accuracy and speed, almost like a calculator. All the villagers were impressed and surprised by the boy's ability with numbers.

Had fate already decided then that this boy would be responsible for preparing textbooks for computer studies in the years to come?

A Fragrant Name

When Balagurusamy was born, he was named Kasthuri. Everyone liked the name. But the child Kasthuri cried continuously without stopping. The elders in the village decided that the name troubled the child. So, his parents changed his name to Balagurusamy. And the boy stopped crying!

Kasthuri, or musk, has a sweet, strong fragrance which can fill the area with its sweet smell. It is no wonder that Balagurusamy's fame spread over the whole world like the fragrance of Kasthuri. The second name that was his—Balagurusamy—belonged to Lord Subrahmanya. The Lord had assimilated all knowledge even as a child and could even impart the meaning of 'OHM' to his father, Lord Paramasiva.

Does this not answer the eternal question, 'What is in a name?'

Meanwhile, a middle school for students from sixth to eighth standard was inaugurated in a nearby village soon after Balagurusamy had started working in the shop. Balagurusamy wanted to join the sixth standard in the school, but Muthusamy, the shop owner, vehemently opposed it. He even threatened the boy's father against sending him to school. The shopkeeper had his personal reasons for keeping the boy with him. Where else would he get such an efficient worker for his shop?

Balagurusamy had to mask his disappointment and continue to work in the shop that year, thus losing one year of study.

E. Balagurusamy studying in a verandah school in his village, Andipattikottai, Tamil Nadu

Balagurusamy went to the middle school to seek admission in the sixth standard in May 1956. Another problem awaited him there. Balagurusamy could not produce a certificate to prove that he had completed the fifth standard. But help appeared in the form of a teacher named Chandrasekhar. The teacher was also the headmaster of the school. He recognized Balagurusamy's brilliance and had him admitted in the school in the sixth standard.

Balagurusamy's mind was never restricted to what was taught in the classroom or was in the prescribed textbooks. As he started growing up, the villagers soon grew to envy him as well.

4
Street Light to Limelight

Feel not frustrated saying, 'Tis hard'
He who tries, attain(s) striving's reward

—Thirukkural 611

'What? He wants to go to school! What good will it be if he studies? Shouldn't he be working in the field?'

Many of the jealous residents of Andipattikottai village expressed such sentiments when they saw that Balagurusamy was attending the school in their village. Many of the villagers could not stand the thought of a boy from a financially weak and poor family aspiring to better things in life through education.

If the boy had become despondent after hearing such words from these malicious villagers, the world would have lost a man who worked tirelessly for the welfare of society. The students of computer science across the world would not have had the privilege of being taught by an eminent teacher named Prof. Balagurusamy. The UPSC that conducts the civil services examinations in India would have lost the services of a distinguished scholar. The Andhra Pradesh government would not have had the advantage of having such a scholarly adviser for the application of Computers and Information Technology in its administration. The Rajasthan and the Punjab governments would have been denied the services of an outstanding scholar—as the Development Consultant for Science and Technology. We would not have had Dr Balagurusamy as the vice-chancellor of Anna University, the most significant technological university in the country.

This boy would not have had the chance to help the students of information technology (IT) and computer science by writing more than forty textbooks, which went on to form part of the syllabus for many universities. These books would not have been translated into various languages worldwide. His name would not have headed the list of eminent scholars of IT in Asia.

Later, as an expert in object-oriented technology, artificial intelligence (AI) and expert systems, quality management in education, business process re-engineering, educational administration and management, e-governance and other fields, Dr Balagurusamy would not have travelled all over the world, participating in discussions and conferences. Many would have been in the dark about the new National Education Policy 2020 as Dr Balagurusamy would not have been in a position to give us the gist of the policy in a language that all can understand.

It is a well-known fact of history that time blesses the world with some extraordinarily brilliant minds every now and then. This alone can be the reason behind the unique versatility of Dr Balagurusamy.

'If you give them too much education, they will no longer respect elders' was what some of the villagers feared. There was an astrologer who strongly supported such beliefs. He spread the cowry shells of his trade and declared that Balagurusamy would be bad in mathematics, and education was not forecast in his horoscope. So he advised Ellappa Naicker not to waste his money by providing further education for his son.

The father was in a dilemma. Naturally, the parents wanted their son to be with them throughout their lives. But fate had something else in store.

Balagurusamy was the fifth child of Ellappa Naicker and Thambayammal. He had an elder brother, three elder sisters and a sister younger to him. All his sisters were married and had settled in nearby villages and were leading happy lives. His elder brother Perumal was living in Andipattikottai, and was engaged in agricultural work. Perumal stood firm with his younger brother, even as the villagers discouraged the young boy. He reassured him, 'I am here to look after the cattle and work in the fields. You concentrate on your studies.'

Andipattikottai was an agricultural village consisting of about fifty families. The street lamps were lit using kerosene. While Balagurusamy was in the village, there were no cinema theatres, celebrations of festivals or any competitions in arts or sports there. During the drought of the 1950s, Karur district was severely affected. Cultivation came to a standstill. Balagurusamy's father had considerable land, but as water availability for irrigation stopped, he too was in distress. Most of the men who used to work in the fields started doing manual labour in the wealthy households or went to work in the estates. Some fed their families by tending cattle for others and even looking after small children.

The elders in Balagurusamy's house did not want him to do any work. They wanted him to concentrate on his studies. Still, Balagurusamy contributed as much as he could to the upkeep of the family. Early in the morning, he would head out to perform manual labour that would earn him some wages. After attending his classes, he would work on the farm. As night fell, he would be on the platform near the village temple, where he could read his lessons under the light of the street lamp. As members of his family were all at home, there was no place for him to study. So he would study under the street lamps late into the night and go to sleep on the platform itself. Early the next morning, he would go home and start his daily routine again. This was how Balagurusamy studied till he completed his SSLC (Secondary School Leaving Certificate) examination.

Balagurusamy came first in all the school examinations. The students who scored good marks were eligible to contest for election as School Pupil Leader (SPL) when they were in the eighth standard. Balagurusamy decided to compete. His opponent was the son of a rich man in the village. When the boy heard that Balagurusamy, who was from an impoverished family, had dared to contest against him, he was enraged. But it was Balagurusamy who won and became the school leader.

It was stipulated that the SPL would have to step down if any complaints were raised against him. Of course, the boy would have to suffer disgrace too.

The boy who lost to Balagurusamy was waiting for a chance to hit back at him. There was a small shop in front of the school. The owner used to entrust the shop to Balagurusamy when he had to go somewhere. The shop stocked some sweets, pencils and things that schoolchildren needed. One day, when Balagurusamy was looking after the shop, a torchlight was found missing. The rich boy seized the opportunity and accused Balagurusamy of stealing the torch.

The shop owner immediately complained to the headmaster about Balagurusamy without asking him anything about it. The headmaster summoned Balagurusamy and questioned him. But Balagurusamy did not show any fear; he did not flinch or cry. Instead, he made an unexpected statement. 'If it is proved that I have taken the torchlight, I will end my studies and leave the school.'

The teachers were surprised to hear his words. How could a small boy be so bold! The very next day, the owner of the shop came to the headmaster and told him that he had got the torch back.

The shine in Balagurusamy's eyes spoke volumes. If one stuck to the truth, courage would come unaided. This was the first test that Balagurusamy faced in his life, and the first victory of truth.

The public examination for the eighth standard students of the Andipattikottai school was held at a nearby school in the district of Karur. Balagurusamy topped the list of the students who passed the examination. But unlike today, nobody came to know about the students who had achieved meritorious success. The lack of any means of communication made it impossible.

If any student from Andipattikottai wanted to continue his studies, he had to join the ninth standard at the secondary school at Aravakurichi, far away from the village.

Back then, villagers considered someone who had passed the eighth standard 'a well- educated man'. But considering the ability and enthusiasm that Balagurusamy exhibited, passing the eighth standard was nothing sensational.

He was extremely proficient in mathematics, and his mind seemed to work like a computer. Mathematics was but a toy in his hands. How could anyone think of stopping the rise of a genius like this by keeping him from moving beyond the eighth standard? Was it right to restrain the flow of the Ganga into a copper vessel?

E. Balagurusamy studying under the street lamp in his village

The Voice of Social Justice

As Balagurusamy reached home after school, his mother usually kept something aside for him to eat. One day, he brought a friend with him.

'Send your friend away and come and have something to eat,' his mother said.

'We both will eat whatever you have kept for me,' said Balagurusamy.

'Okay. Ask the boy to sit outside...and you come into the kitchen,' his mother instructed him.

Balagurusamy understood that his mother had said this because his friend was from a low-caste family.

'I will only eat if you can serve both of us together...otherwise, I don't want it,' Balagurusamy said in a firm tone. His mother had to serve both of them together.

Balagurusamy's uncle came into the house at that time and saw this.

'Sprinkle cow dung and water everywhere in the house. Then go to the river Kaveri and take a dip in the waters to be saved from the sin of impurity,' he thundered.

But Balagurusamy did not take all this seriously.

'If you want it so much, you may go to the Kaveri and have a bath, Uncle,' he said and ran out of the house with his friend.

The biggest impediment in the path of Balagurusamy's education was his family's poverty. Ellappa Naicker was worried whether he should allow his son to continue his studies. What worried him the most was whether he would be able to afford it. After long deliberations with himself, his father said, 'Now you can end your studies, my son. You are the most learned person in this village. Do some work on the farm and help the family.' Ellappa Naicker sighed as he spoke thus.

Hunger or Honour?

After the board exams were over, Chandrasekhar, the headmaster of the middle school, invited Balagurusamy and another student to his house as they had done well in the examinations. Balagurusamy and the student went to Srirangam, near Trichy, where the house was located.

The headmaster invited them into his home and introduced them to his mother. Then he went out on some urgent work. Though it was time for them to have lunch, the teacher had not returned. Both the boys were starving. So the teacher's mother got ready to serve the food. She asked them to wash their hands at the tap outside and sit on the verandah outside the house.

Balagurusamy could not reconcile himself to being served food on the verandah. He said to his companion, 'Honour is greater than hunger. How can we be treated like this?'

The two boys were out of the headmaster's house and on the bus to their own village within no time. They did not even wait for the teacher to come back!

Balagurusamy, who was eager to continue his studies, was disappointed and did not know what to do. But his elder brother Perumal came to his help again. Perumal said to his father, 'I couldn't study much. Balagurusamy is very intelligent. Let him continue with his studies.'

Avarakurichi was ten kilometres away from Andipattikottai. If Balagurusamy joined the school there, he would have to travel the distance daily by bus. How would they find the money for that? That was the problem.

'I will go to school on a cycle,' Balagurusamy suggested. So when that obstacle had been successfully cleared, Balagurusamy started on his journey to the top, riding a bicycle to the school on a daily basis.

5

On the Wings of Science

*In waiting time, feign peace like a stork.
In fighting time, strike at the peak.*

—Thirukkural 490

Balagurusamy bought a cycle to go to school. He used the small savings he had built up since childhood and the money he had managed to put together by selling the goat he had brought up. He had the support of his elder brother Perumal in all this. But they had not told their father anything about buying the cycle. When Ellappa Naicker came to know about it, he said, 'Who told you to sell the goat? Why did you buy a cycle now?'

Perumal came to his brother's rescue. 'Didn't he buy the cycle with what he had saved, Father? He needs a cycle to go to school. He didn't want to trouble you for that.'

Ellappa Naicker calmed down upon realizing that his son had not asked him for the money. But he had some stipulations for the boy if he were to attend school. Balagurusamy would have to work on the farm before and after school.

A private bus, 'LGB', plied between Karur and Dindigul. That bus passed through Andipattikottai on its return trip to Karur at seven o'clock in the morning. The villagers usually started work in the fields after hearing the sound of the bus passing through their village. But Balagurusamy began to work on the farm from five in the morning. As soon as he heard the bus pass by, he would rush home to have his breakfast and then leave for school on his cycle. The sound of the bus must have helped Balagurusamy keep time, and later punctuality would go on to become an integral part of his character.

While in middle school, Balagurusamy worked part-time in a big grocery shop. This experience helped him. He would go to the shop at 4 p.m. when school ended and work there till 7. On Sundays, when there was no school, he would go to the shop. Balagurusamy saved whatever money he got from this shop. His habit of saving money was something that he held on to and he taught his students the value of saving when he himself became a teacher, eager to lead his students on the path of virtue. He had proved the value of such practices in his own life before advising others about them. Similar to the National Cadet Corps (NCC) organized in the colleges, there were units of NCC organized in schools at that time. There were army, navy and air force wings of the NCC. Balagurusamy wanted to join the army wing, but he was disqualified as he was underweight. But as was his habit, he was undaunted by the rejection and continued to try to join. In the end, he got a chance to join the air force wing of the NCC, even as he continued his studies and his work.

When he reached high school, he had to choose a vocational subject like agriculture or engineering. As he came from a family of farmers, he did not believe he could learn anything new by studying agriculture. So he chose engineering; the other subjects were history, Tamil, English and mathematics. His interest in engineering kept growing, and soon, it became a passion. He received training in building construction, carpentry, electrical work, electronics, turning and fitting and other such techniques that made him proficient in the repair of electrical and electronic equipment.

Balagurusamy developed an interest in social issues when he was in the tenth standard. He was disturbed by the inequality, injustice and the practices of discrimination against some sections of people. At this time, he became attracted to the Dravida Munnetra Kazhagam (DMK), a political party established in the 1950s in Tamil Nadu. He started listening to the inspiring words of Arignar Annadurai, Kalaignar Karunanidhi and Navalar Nedunchezhiyan. As he was the school leader, he invited some of these leaders to the school to address the students. But none of the leaders, though it may seem difficult to believe in the present day, spoke about politics when they were within the premises of the school. Instead they focused on the Tamil language, culture and history.

Balagurusamy was especially inspired by the speeches of Navalar Nedunchezhiyan, who had deep knowledge of many issues and was known as a walking encyclopedia. During his speech, he quoted a couplet from the *Thirukkural*.

> *Falsehood may take the place of truthful word,*
> *If blessing, free from fault, it can afford.**
>
> —Thirukkural 292

With a story, Nedunchezhiyan explained the meaning of these lines. Once, a good and pious man was being followed by some people intent on killing him. The man took shelter in the hermitage of a sage. The sage knew this man to be noble and also that a group of murderers was following him.

When the men came upon the hermitage, they asked the sage, 'Swamiji, have you seen the man we were chasing?'

The sage did not want to reveal the truth. 'No one has come this way,' he said. The men believed the words of the sage and left the place. And so, the chased man escaped death.

Balagurusamy was impressed by these lines of the *Thirukkural* that Nedunchezhiyan had recited.

On another occasion, E.V. Ramasami Naicker (popularly known as Thanthai Periyar) addressed the students. Balagurusamy was mesmerised by the words that he spoke. 'Don't become lazy by believing in God and religion. Instead, you must have faith in your knowledge and the readiness to do hard work. Only with that will you be able to achieve success in life. If you make it your life's motto to share what you have with others, then there is no need to believe in God or go to any temple. Young men should not be like the bull tethered to an oil press. They should be ready to try new things. Only then will they be able to eradicate all superstitions from society and bring prosperity. Students should cultivate knowledge and wisdom and work for the prosperity of the people and the country.'

---

*Thirukkural, *Thirukkural: English Translation and Commentary*, G.U Pope (trans.), CreateSpace Independent Publishing Platform, 31 August 2017.

While these Dravidian values were held in high regard by Balagurusamy, he was equally concerned about the state of the nation. One of the camps for the cadets of the air force wing of the NCC was being held at Sulur, near Coimbatore, which had an airbase. Some of the topics discussed during the camp focused on the way one should behave in society, the importance of discipline in life and the honour of serving one's country by joining the armed forces. In another such camp, held at Madras the following year, Education Minister C. Subramaniam addressed the students. He became the guiding light of Balagurusamy's future.

Balagurusamy also started reading *The Hindu* in the ninth standard. The newspaper would be delivered at home for a monthly payment of five rupees. Upon perusing the newspaper one day, Balagurusamy realized that he had achieved an admirable distinction in the tenth standard examination. The whole family was delighted.

After this, he would have to go through a one-year intermediate course before joining a college for a degree course. Balagurusamy's father wanted to do something for his son as he was proud of his achievement. He consulted the president of the local panchayat and the local Member of the Legislative Assembly (MLA), and together they met the district educational officer. The district educational officer declared that Balagurusamy was qualified to become a teacher. He had passed the SSLC examination with high marks, and so he promised to appoint him as an untrained teacher in a primary school.

Ellappa Naicker was exhilarated to hear it. He shared the good news with his family and villagers with great pride.

6
Forever Optimistic

A psychic heart is a wealth indeed.
Worldly wealth departs in speed.

—Thirukkural 592

Balagurusamy was not without regrets when his father asked him to start working. His father had told him that the school was thinking of offering him a job as a teacher. But he was still worried as it seemed to be just a promise, and he was aware that a job like this was not so easy for someone like him. He saw no other way to support his family who were in a difficult situation. He was in a dilemma about where he would go now, and he even thought of going back to work in the fields.

But as Rabindranath Tagore has said, 'I cannot choose the best. The best chooses me.' These words echoed in Balagurusamy's mind. So he waited.

He went to the school to collect his certificates and the marksheet. The headmaster of the Aravakurichi High School was Thomas Lourdesamy. After collecting the marksheet and the transfer certificate from the office, all the students had to meet him. When Balagurusamy met the headmaster, some of his other teachers—Abdul Jabbar, C. Srinivasan, Khader Moideen and K.R. Ramasamy—were in the room. Balagurusamy stood there with a troubled mind.

The headmaster called him in and asked, 'What is your plan now, Balaguru?'

'I plan to start working on the farm,' the answer came immediately.

'Why?' asked the headmaster, disappointment apparent in his voice.

'The main reason is the lack of money, Sir. We don't have the money to pay the fees if I decide to study further. So I think I should work in the fields and support my family,' answered Balagurusamy.

'You have topped the list of students of this district in the SSLC examination. You have brought credit to this school through this. You should study further. So your decision...' The headmaster stopped. Balagurusamy just stood there, looking down at the floor. The headmaster, too, was thinking of how he could do something to help the best student of his school...the one who should study further but was unable to do so. The boy stood there as all the others got their certificates and left the room. Balagurusamy was the last to receive the credentials from the headmaster.

As the headmaster signed the conduct certificate, he sincerely prayed to Jesus to show the boy the right way in life. These were the words that he wrote on the certificate:

'Very regular, holds the first rank in school. Deserves encouragement.'

Khader Moideen, his science teacher, said, 'Balaguru, you are a lion among students. I have been struck with wonder upon watching your speed in solving mathematical problems. And the steps you take to do that. You are so bright. You should become an engineer. Shower thy mercy on him, O Allah!' he prayed.

'May Lord Muruga bless you,' said Srinivasan, his mathematics teacher.

As he was returning home, Balagurusamy thought about his science teacher who had advised him to study engineering. He waited eagerly to show his certificates to his father and tell him of this new desire.

But his father's words gave him a shock. 'Balaguru, you have done very well in your examination. Now you have the best education in our village. You have been offered a job as a teacher. So you will have to go for that soon.'

'Father,' Balagurusamy said, 'I wish to study further. All my teachers also want me to do that.'

His father's face reddened in anger. 'I have made all the arrangements for your job. The panchayat has taken the decision. So how can you say this now?'

Once again, his elder brother came to his aid. 'Let him study, Father. Why should we prevent such an intelligent boy from studying further?'

In *The Hindu*, Balagurusamy saw advertisements for admission into PSG Polytechnic, Coimbatore and Alagappa Polytechnic, Karaikudi. He submitted his applications to both colleges. As he had very high marks, he was called for an interview by both these places. Many buses plied the roads between Karur and Coimbatore in those days, so Balagurusamy chose to join PSG College there.

Despite the pleadings of both the sons, their father did not relent. He was pretty firm in his decision. 'I cannot spend money to send you to college. I have got you a job as a teacher. Take up that job,' he said.

The brothers thought of many ways to find the money for Balagurusamy to join PSG College. At last, they hit upon a plan. He would not need the cycle when he went to Coimbatore. It was a Hercules cycle which was in great demand in those days. Moreover, many people had their eyes on Balagurusamy's cycle. The villagers believed that Balagurusamy could do well in his studies as he had gone to school on that 'lucky' cycle. Many offered to buy it. A prominent member of the community, known as Aalamarathupatti Goundar, bought the bicycle for his son and paid a good price for it to Balagurusamy.

But when Balagurusamy reached home, his father was furious with him.

7
Hard Work Pays

Fortune enquires, enters with boom
Where tireless strivers have their home

—Thirukkural 594

'Why did you sell the cycle?' Ellappa Naicker boomed when his son returned home.

'You told me that you would not be able to find the money for me to join the college. So what else could I do?' Balagurusamy answered with no show of defiance in his words.

Ellappa Naicker could see the sense of purpose and determination in his son. But he could not control his anger when he knew that the boy had sold the cycle without his knowledge. He had felt the same way when Balagurusamy had sold the goat to buy the bicycle. Balagurusamy, too, understood that this outburst was a natural right that his father had over him.

Ellappa Naicker's anger did not last long. Though he was not in the habit of talking a lot with his son, his love for the boy was strong and evident. The father had nothing against his son wanting to pursue higher studies. Money was the only thing that stood as a significant barrier before the loving father. Balagurusamy, too, knew that. But his mind continued to hold steadfast. 'Never go back until you have achieved your goal. Be persistent in your efforts,' he thought to himself.

Balagurusamy went to Coimbatore to attend the interview at PSG College. His friend Venkatasamy was also with him. Boys in college were supposed to wear full trousers. Instead of the mandated trousers, Balagurusamy had managed to get cheap cotton full-length trousers for use in the college. They found a room at Seetharam Lodge near the railway station.

> **Save to Save Yourself!**
>
> *Dr Balagurusamy always advised his students about the necessity of developing the habit of saving money. He visited his old school at Aravakurichi in 2016 with Thiru. Sengettuvan, correspondent,[*] Valluvar College, Karur. There, he spoke about the importance of developing the habit of savings. 'Even if it is a small amount, students should learn to keep it and deposit it in a bank.' He reminded them that it would be helpful when they had to go to college later. 'I used the money I had saved in my childhood for my education,' he told the students. He then paid for about a hundred students to start their own bank accounts.*

They reached the college in time for the interview. The PSG Polytechnic and the PSG Engineering College were located in the same compound. Both the institutions were under the control of the same principal. Balagurusamy met Prof. Ramasamy, the work shop superintendent, with his interview card. Prof. Ramasamy was in charge of the admissions to the Polytechnic. The professor asked Balagurusamy something in English, but Balagurusamy, who had studied in Tamil medium, could not understand it. But the professor was excited to see the marksheet that Balagurusamy had given him. He said to Balagurusamy, 'Do not worry. You are selected; you can now pay the fee and join the college.'

This happened when all the other students were waiting for the interview. Balagurusamy was happy that he had been selected without an interview, but there was a problem.

'Sir, I have not brought enough money to pay now. I will have to go home and get the money.'

The principal and correspondent of the college, Prof. G.R. Damodaran, was one of the great contributors to engineering education in India. He was also present at the college at that time. He believed that a promising student should never be denied education and he

---

[*]Correspondent refers to the owner of a private college in Tamil Nadu. If the college is run by a trust, a representative of the trust is referred to as the correspondent.

took the initiative to give special consideration to the sons of teachers and farmers in college admissions. Balagurusamy qualified for this consideration. The remark made by the headmaster in the conduct certificate also left an impression. 'Very regular, holds the first rank in school. Deserves encouragement.'

So as per the advice of Prof. G.R. Damodaran, Prof. Ramasamy instructed Balagurusamy to pay whatever he had with him and the rest later.

Thus, Balagurusamy became a student of PSG Polytechnic. When he returned home, he had to face his father's anger. Still, his brother Perumal supported him in every possible way.

Now he had to find the money to pay the rest of the fees. He had to pay the hostel fees and the college fees within fifteen days. He was not sure if his father would give him the money. But his brother assured him that their father would forget his anger by then and provide him with the amount. Under Perumal's persuasion, Ellappa Naicker took a loan of a hundred rupees from a moneylender. He got only ninety rupees as ten rupees had been deducted in advance as interest. He would have to pay back ten rupees a week for ten weeks. As Balagurusamy left for Coimbatore, his mind was disturbed as he had now become the cause for making his father a debtor.

There were two impediments before him as he joined the college. The first was poverty, and the second was his inability to understand the lessons which were taught in English. He had no problems with mathematics, physics and chemistry classes. But as the classes were all in English, he started feeling desperate. He thought that he would never be able to master the language. He felt that he was wasting his father's money because he might fail due to a lack of proficiency in the language.

Two months passed. Balagurusamy decided that he would discontinue his studies and go home. He approached Prof. Venkatasubramanian, his mathematics teacher, and spoke to him about his decision. The professor, who was teaching calculus, listened patiently to the boy speaking about his difficulties. Then he made a suggestion. 'Now, you have been here for two months. You will have quarterly examinations in about a month. Write that examination, and then you can go home.'

'Should I write an examination just to face failure, Sir?' Balagurusamy asked.

'You write the examination first. Then we will decide what is to be done.'

Balagurusamy could say nothing.

In the Ramayana, Jambavan, the king of the bears, makes Anjaneya, a mighty monkey, aware of his power and makes him jump over the ocean to reach Lanka. Prof. Venkatasubramanian was the Jambavaan who realized the potential in the Anjaneya that he saw in Balagurusamy.

Balagurusamy found it difficult to converse in English. But he could write in English. Prof. Venkatasubramanian had seen how the boy had answered the questions in the science subjects in English.

As soon as the examinations were over, Balagurusamy approached Prof. Venkatasubramanian again. 'Sir, I have written the examinations. Now I am going home.'

'Wait for one more week. You will get the answer papers by then. Get them, and then you can go,' the professor instructed him.

Another week passed. Prof. Venkatasubramanian, the maths teacher, came to the class with the answer papers that he had valued. The students waited with bated breath as the names were called, one after the other, and the marks were announced. Balagurusamy's name was not called till the end, but he remained calm.

Balagurusamy thought that his name was not being called as he must have failed miserably. At last, the professor called out his name. 'Balagurusamy.'

Balagurusamy approached the professor with no emotions as he had already decided to quit his studies. Then the professor quietly announced to the class. 'Balagurusamy has come first in this class.'

As Balagurusamy stood there, unable to believe his ears, the professor held him, patting him on the back. The boy looked up, and he heard a thousand words in the smiling face of his teacher. Balagurusamy felt his eyes brimming with tears.

'Now, what do you say? Do you still want to go home?'

Balagurusamy couldn't say anything.

The papers contained questions for 150 marks for mathematics and other science subjects. Students could try to answer as many questions as possible and get more than 100 marks. No other student in the class had got more than 70, but Balagurusamy had scored 140! With this, all his hopes were revived. He started pursuing his studies with determination.

But soon, financial difficulties troubled him again. Prof. Venkatasubramanian found a solution for that too.

'You are eligible for a scholarship. You will get the scholarship offered by the central government based on the income of your family and the marks you have scored. That will meet all your expenses,' he told Balagurusamy. He explained the details of the 'Merit cum Means Scholarship' and how he was to apply for it. Applications were invited by the end of August. The students had to submit the marksheets of the SSLC examination and the quarterly examination held in the college. They had to submit an Income Certificate issued by an officer not below the rank of a tahsildar. But it had to be submitted within two weeks.

Balagurusamy collected the form and started for home in great excitement. He wanted to tell his father that he would not need to take any more loans to educate him. He could almost imagine how happy his father would be. He would just have to get the Income Certificate and submit the application on time.

But here again, he was confronted with difficulties. The tahsildar would issue the certificate based on a recommendation made by the chief of the gramsabha. However, the chief of the gramsabha was among those who were envious of Balagurusamy; he was against the family of Ellappa Naicker because Balagurusamy had joined college. He refused to give the letter of recommendation. Someone in the village suggested that Balagurusamy should directly approach the tahsildar in Karur.

Balagurusamy reached Karur and waited till 3 p.m. to meet the tahsildar. Unfortunately, he too was firm that he would not sign the form unless he got the letter of recommendation from the chief of the gramsabha.

Balagurusamy could only shed tears of helplessness as he stood outside the tahsildar's office. One man saw him standing there with tears streaming down his face. The man asked him, 'Why are you crying, my boy?'

Balagurusamy explained everything.

'Is that all? Just give ten rupees to the tahsildar, and he will sign the form immediately,' the man said.

The boy almost burst with anger and disappointment upon hearing this. 'So even students have to pay bribes! Where is justice in this? This should be stopped,' said the boy, boiling with anger.

Balagurusamy had just enough money for the bus fare back to Coimbatore. So, what was he to do?

The man who had suggested paying the bribe came up to Balagurusamy and asked, 'What happened? Don't you have the money to give the tahsildar?'

As Balagurusamy said nothing, the man pointed to a house on the opposite side of the road. 'That is the Sub-Collector's house. If he signs the form, your problem will be over. Why don't you try your luck?'

Balagurusamy thought, 'What will happen if he too refuses?'

Still, he went to the house. The board read: 'P.B. Krishnasamy, IAS, Sub-Collector'.

The officer had just come back from office. The guard at the gate did not allow Balagurusamy to go in.

'You can meet him only in the office, not at home,' he said.

A Shining Memory

P.B. Krishnasamy, aged 85, now lives at Adayar in Chennai after serving in the central and state governments. He still remembers the incident that happened 59 years ago. 'Who should get such a certificate if not a boy who had scored such good marks? I followed Balagurusamy's career as he went up the ladder. I used to admire his courage and his contributions to the field of education. My daughter worked as a teacher at Anna University when Prof. Balagurusamy was the vice-chancellor.

'I also remember when a girl came to me for a Nativity Certificate. This happened after I had met Balagurusamy. I

asked the girl how I would know if she belonged to that place. She immediately said, "Would a student lie when she comes for a certificate?" I saw the truth in the question that she raised.'

'No, I want to see him now. It is very urgent,' Balagurusamy said, gathering courage.

This led to a minor fracas with the gatekeeper. The sub-collector's wife came out to see what was happening.

'What is going on here?' she asked.

'Tomorrow is the last date for submitting this application at Coimbatore. I need Sir's signature for it,' Balagurusamy explained in a choked voice.

When she understood the urgency of the matter, she allowed him to come inside.

Soon, the sub-collector came out as his wife had informed him of the incident.

'Sit down,' he said and offered some water to Balagurusamy.

He went through the papers, including the marksheets. He signed the document, stamped the office seal himself, handed it over to Balagurusamy and said, 'All the best.'

Balagurusamy thanked him with folded hands. His mind now cleared like the sky after a downpour. It was six o'clock in the evening. He had to run—no, fly—to the bus stand to catch the last bus to Coimbatore.

8
Anti-Hindi Agitation

Do with a firm will, though pains beset,
the deed that brings delight at last.

—Thirukkural 669

Balagurusamy managed to submit the application for the central government scholarship along with all the necessary papers on the last day. The receipt of the application was acknowledged a few days later. Now his mind was at peace and he started feeling more confident and proud of his achievements.

There were five different categories of hostel messes in the college—'A', 'B', 'C', 'D' and 'E'. 'A' and 'C' messes were for vegetarians. 'B' and 'D' were for those who wanted non-vegetarian food. 'E' was for those who were economically backward. The students used to call the 'E' mess an 'Economic' mess. 'E' mess charges were less (90 paise only) while in the other categories, the prices were more than one rupee. Remember, this was at the beginning of the 1960s. Balagurusamy decided to dine in the 'E' mess throughout his time at the college.

He wrote to his father and told him that he would not have to take out any more loan for his education as he had found other means of meeting all the expenses.

Once his financial needs were met by the scholarship, he found greater joy in his academic life. Many of his classmates and juniors approached him for help with lessons. Balagurusamy too enjoyed helping them. This made him a prominent figure in the college.

Gradually, his difficulty with speaking and writing in English also disappeared. And he continued to be the first in every examination!

E. Balagurusamy participating in the anti-Hindi agitation of Tamil Nadu

Balagurusamy and 'E'

There is much in common between 'E', the fifth letter of the alphabet, and Prof. Balagurusamy. Balagurusamy dined in the 'E' mess throughout his studies. He was 'E'xcellent in his career from day one. He is a well-known 'E'ducationist. He chose 'E'lectrical in his 'E'ngineering studies. And he took up the first assignment in BHEL in the department of 'E'nergy Systems. Balagurusamy strongly believes in 'E'nvironmental protection, and he made Anna University a plastic-free campus. He also advocates strong 'E'thics.

As PSG Engineering College and PSG Polytechnic were in the same compound, they had a combined students' union, which worked in an exemplary manner. The chairman of the union was from the Engineering College and the vice chairman from the Polytechnic. The secretary was usually a student of the Engineering College while the joint secretary would be from the Polytechnic. During the final year of his studies, Balagurusamy was elected as the joint secretary. The management of the college provided the funds required for the activities of the union. The students never misused this fund, and the college authorities were happy with the union's activities.

The anti-Hindi agitation during the 1960s led to considerable repercussions in Tamil Nadu's political field. Students played a significant role in this agitation. In a way, it could even be said that it was only because of the students that the agitation achieved success. The students were angry with C. Subramanian and O.V. Alagesan, both ministers in the Union Cabinet at that time, for their role in forcing Hindi on the people of Tamil Nadu. Both these ministers were closely associated with PSG College. Still, when they arrived in Coimbatore during the agitation, the students of PSG College held a protest at the airport by presenting themselves with hair shaved off. But Balagurusamy, who did not believe in such gimmicks, did not participate in this protest held at the airport.

The correspondent of PSG College, Prof. G.R. Damodaran, allowed the students under him to take part in the agitation against the imposition of Hindi in Tamil Nadu. But Thiru. Avinashilingam Chettiar, correspondent of the Ramakrishna Polytechnic at Periyanaiken Palayam in Coimbatore, did not allow the students to participate in the agitation. He ordered the closure of the hostel mess when some students joined the protest, and they were denied food from there. This incited the students to intensify the protest against the management of Ramakrishna Polytechnic.

'None Can Touch Me'

It is customary in Tamil Nadu to have the hair of a child shaved and have his ear lobes pierced during infancy. But Balagurusamy's parents could not perform this rite for him. Balagurusamy refused to have his hair removed and his ears pierced when he was older. And the ceremony has not been performed till date.

When asked about this, Prof. Balagurusamy says with a smile, 'None can ever tonsure my hair or pierce my ears at any time.'

True, no one has ever been able to make Balagurusamy do anything against his genuine beliefs.

As a part of this intensified agitation, the students stopped many trains. As the joint secretary of the students' union at PSG, Balagurusamy led this agitation. They hijacked the Coimbatore-Mettupalayam passenger train and reached Periyanaiken Palayam at 6.30 p.m. The district collector, Ramanathan, and principal, G.R. Damodaran, went to the site and tried to intervene and find an amicable solution. But the students were not ready to relent.

The students pointed out their grievance. 'The anti-Hindi agitation in Tamil Nadu has come to the notice of people all over India. College authorities all over the state have permitted students to be a part of the agitation. How can Ramakrishna College alone refuse such permission and persecute the students staying in the college hostel? They are paying fees to stay and have meals there.'

Ragging Month

Ragging was a method used by institutions to familiarize those who are newly admitted to the atmosphere of the institution. Alas, over the years the practice has been distorted, perpetuating violence and discrimination instead of a healthy camaraderie among students. Prof. Balagurusamy, however, believes that ragging, in its essence, is not a bad custom.

'We must remember that ragging, which has been banned now, had been allowed and even welcomed at one time. At the PSG College of Technology, ragging was allowed during the first month. This was done with the permission of the management. Students benefited from such ragging in those days. It was meant to help the students gain self-confidence. It allowed the students to mingle, know, love and cooperate with one another. This was also an occasion to bring out the hidden talents of the new students. The seniors would make the juniors do some work in a spirit of camaraderie. This helped those from the rural areas shed their shyness and move with the others. Of course, any student involved in overdoing it would be warned and, if necessary, punished suitably. After a month of ragging, the seniors would help the newcomers by giving them books and other study materials.'

Prof. G.R. Damodaran felt that what they were saying was just, and he approached the management of Ramakrishna College to come to an amicable settlement. The effort bore fruit, and the hostel was reopened. Food was also provided to the students. The correspondent, Avinashilingam Chettiar, met the students and expressed his regret for whatever had happened.

The agitation was brought to a close. While the students were coming back to Coimbatore city, they destroyed all the signboards written in Hindi on the way. Balagurusamy was at the forefront of this agitation in January 1965, but when the final year examinations were held in April 1965, he still retained the first rank.

9

In Love with Electricity

*No foe defies the speaker clear,
flawless, puissant, and free from fear.*

—Thirukkural 647

Ask Prof. Balagurusamy what his favourite occupation is, and, even in his sleep he will give only one answer: 'Teaching!' It seems to be engraved even in his DNA.

'One need not be a teacher by profession to be an educator. When one passes on to others what knowledge one has got so that they can benefit from it, it is also teaching,' Prof. Balagurusamy often says so, and his life illustrates his beliefs.

Balagurusamy finished his diploma in engineering at PSG Polytechnic and returned to his village in May 1965. The fresh smell of his village soil and the cool breeze energized him. Now he had to decide what he would do next.

From *The Hindu* he learnt that he had passed the diploma examination with a first class, as he had expected. He went to his college to get the marksheet. Prof. Jayaraman, the head of the department of electrical engineering, was happy to see the excellent marks that the Balagurusamy had scored. 'So, what is your plan now, Balaguru?' asked the professor.

'I have not made any specific plan, Sir,' said Balagurusamy.

It was clear from his expression that he wanted to pursue higher studies, but the conditions at home were not favourable.

At the time, the book *Problems in Electrical Engineering* by Parker Smith was popular among electrical engineering students. The text was full of problems to be worked out. There were about twelve chapters, each covering topics on electrical circuits, transmission, distribution, electrical machines, alternating-current machines, direct-current machines, etc. Twenty to twenty-five problems were included in each topic. The answers to these problems were also given in the book. But the method to arrive at the solutions was not provided. The purpose of this book was to test the logical and creative capacities of students as they tried to solve these problems in electrical engineering. For any problem, there could be different ways in which one could arrive at the answer. It was most important that the procedure be brief so that one could arrive at the solutions quickly. Balagurusamy had found the shortest methods to arrive at the correct answers for almost all the problems given in that book. Even the students in the MTech course were not able to do so.

Prof. Jayaraman had known about this unique ability of Balagurusamy. The professor had also seen other students approaching Balagurusamy for help and had observed how efficiently Balagurusamy could clear their doubts. When he heard Balagurusamy giving a vague answer to his question about the future, the professor took him to meet the correspondent. After listening to Jayaraman and seeing the marks scored by Balagurusamy, Prof. Damodaran, the correspondent, also asked him the same question.

'I am interested in the design of electrical systems and machines. I have heard that the famous company GEC recruits engineers quite regularly. I would like to apply for a job there or in some other similar companies,' Balagurusamy revealed his intentions.

The correspondent held some discussion with Prof. Jayaraman and then turned to Balagurusamy and said, 'You are appointed as an instructor in the Polytechnic.'

This was a challenge for Balagurusamy. It was not clear whether he was more excited or surprised to hear these words. He had never thought about a teaching job. A new life beckoned him now. On the 1st of September 1965, Balagurusamy joined PSG Polytechnic as a teacher at the age of nineteen! Everyone in the electrical engineering department was delighted to see Balagurusamy as a teacher but wondered how this boy, a teenager, would confront the students in the class?

In those days, someone from among the office staff usually took attendance before the teachers came to the class. Breaking this tradition, Balagurusamy went to his first class with the attendance register in his hands. The students thought he was someone from the office. As Balagurusamy wished them 'Good Morning' with a smile on his face, they returned the greeting with hesitation.

It took some time for the students to realize that the young man who stood before them was their new teacher.

The students in that class were special, in a way. Most of them were sons of the textile mill owners of Coimbatore. There were more than 600 textile mills in Coimbatore at that time and the owners wanted their sons to be qualified to take charge of the mills and had sent them to PSG College. A diploma in textile technology was meant mainly for these boys. Balagurusamy was to teach them electrical engineering. Students, especially boys, are inclined to be naughty. This is more the case if the boys come from wealthy families. Many teachers found it challenging to manage these students. So there was worry about what a young teacher would face.

It was to such a class that Balagurusamy had come with a smile and a confident 'Good Morning'.

There was an uneasy silence in the classroom as Balagurusamy started calling out the names and marking attendance. As each boy stood up, Balagurusamy made some enquiries and observed the student's body language. Once he had finished taking the attendance and talking to each of them, he addressed the students in a firm but friendly voice.

'Only those who are interested in studying this subject need to sit in my class. Others can go out now. If you want your attendance to be marked, you can come to my room later. But I don't want any disturbance in my class.'

The students were surprised. Generally, teachers would get angry when the boys disturbed the class and ask them to get out. The students would go out, unfazed, almost happily. But they had never seen a teacher who offered to give them attendance even if they did not remain in the class.

Balagurusamy's novel and firm stand reaped rich dividends. All the students attended his classes and paid rapt attention to what was being taught. The other teachers were impressed by this approach that Balagurusamy had taken. Though he had offered to give them attendance, none approached him. Every student remained in the class without causing any disturbance.

Balagurusamy had realized the main drawbacks in forging relationships between the students and the teachers. One was that the teachers failed to make the students understand the lessons well. This denied the students a chance to apply their intelligence to what was being taught. Second, the teachers did not make an attempt to know the students personally. He tried his best to do both. Balagurusamy encouraged students to look for their own ways to find answers to problems while he explained the lessons. His way of associating himself with his students led to a sea change in the boys' attitude. They saw him as an elder brother rather than as a teacher. The students found that they could approach him freely to clear their doubts. Naturally, Balagurusamy became the beloved teacher of the students in no time.

Balagurusamy's method of teaching was also unique. He would explain even the most difficult portions in simple words. At the same time, he would present it attractively. This was an eye-opener for the other teachers too. Balagurusamy explained the law and concept of electrical engineering, emphasizing how these theories could be utilized in practical, everyday life. The students preferred this method.

Understand Before You Do

'Students should try hard to find the solutions to the problems in mathematics by themselves. They should use their intelligence without depending on the teachers. I introduced this system in all the colleges when I was the vice-chancellor. When they find methods of solving problems independently, their innovative power increases, along with that, their ability to think and chart new paths also becomes better,' says Dr Balagurusamy.

He believes in the Chinese dictum 'I hear, I forget. I see, I remember. I do, I understand'. He says that this method certainly

> *improves the thinking ability of students. If a student had to use four steps to solve a problem in the first attempt, the next time, he will only take three steps. This is the secret of Balagurusamy's work.*

Balagurusamy never made notes prior to the classes. He was confident of his deep knowledge of the subject. He also encouraged students to ask non-academic questions related to the topic they were studying. He would then give them detailed and precise answers. He also never tried to avoid answering questions when he was unsure of the answers. He would promise to give the answers the next day. This experience must have been behind the advice that Balagurusamy used to give teachers later in his life: 'Do not teach from your head; teach from your heart.'

ASSOCIATE MEMBER OF INSTITUTE OF ENGINEERS

Although Balagurusamy was seriously involved in teaching and enjoyed the company and friendship of his colleagues, he was troubled as he thought about the fact that he lacked a BE degree. As the department of electrical engineering was common for both the Engineering College and Polytechnic, many of his colleagues had BE and ME degrees. He had only a diploma in engineering.

There is a scheme available where aspiring students can get an Associate Member of Institute of Engineers (AMIE) degree instead of the BE degree. Balagurusamy appeared for this examination while working as an instructor at the Polytechnic. As in the case of the chartered accountancy course, a student had to take all-India examinations at different levels—A, B and C—to get the AMIE degree. Balagurusamy cleared each level in one attempt with high marks and completed all the three levels by November 1969. Indeed, it was a rare feat as AMIE examinations are usually very tough and people generally make three to four attempts to complete each level and take six to ten years to finish the entire programme. Only around 10 per cent of those who appear for the examinations clear them.

But since the AMIE is equivalent to BE degree, Balagurusamy was promoted to the position of Senior Instructor and was also appointed as one of the hostel wardens.

THE FIRST BOOK—CYCLOSTYLED!

In 1970, a new subject, telephony and telegraphy, was introduced in the electronics and communication engineering (ECE) branch at the PSG College of Technology. By that time, G.R. Damodaran had retired and Prof. R. Subbayyan had taken charge as principal. The teachers with BE and ME degrees were not ready to teach this new subject. Prof. Subbayyan was earlier the Head of the department of electrical engineering. Therefore, knowing and trusting the intellectual ability and sincerity of Balagurusamy, Prof. Subbayyan asked him to take up the responsibility of teaching telephony and telegraphy to BE students.

'Sir, this is a subject for the students of the Engineering College. I am an instructor at the Polytechnic. How can I accept this responsibility?' Balagurusamy asked.

But Prof. Subbayyan did not relent. He went on persuading Balagurusamy to do it.

Balagurusamy pleaded further. 'Sir, I have never even touched a telephone. I do not know even how to hold it. How can I teach students about it?'

'Balaguru, I know you are intelligent and ready to work hard. You will be able to do this. I have full confidence in you...and in you *alone*,' said the principal.

In the end, Balagurusamy had to relent. The main obstacle before him was the lack of textbooks on the subject. After a prolonged search, he found a book in the library titled *Telephony* written by John Atkinson, published by Pitman Publishing in London. Some of the students tried to read the book. Balagurusamy asked them what they had understood about the subject. 'Very difficult, Sir, we did not understand anything from the book,' was the answer he got.

This made Balagurusamy realize that he could solve the problem by simplifying what was in the five-hundred-page book so that the students would understand it. He prepared a booklet 'Telephony and

Telegraphy', explaining the concepts and working principles in a simple and easy-to-understand style. This was the first of the plethora of books that were published by Dr Balagurusamy later.

The technology to make multiple copies of documents had not been developed in those days. The available method was of taking cyclostyled copies. For this, one had to type the matter on a particular type of paper and take copies with the help of a roller spread with ink. Copies of this booklet were taken on the cyclostyling machine and were distributed free of cost to the students at PSG.

As word spread among the student community about a book that explained the complex subject in a simple manner, students from other colleges, like the Coimbatore Institute of Technology and Guindy Engineering College, Chennai, came to PSG to get Balagurusamy's notes. The cooperative store at the PSG College of Technology sold many copies of the booklet for five rupees each.

The First Royalty

Prof. Velliyangiri, who was in charge of the cooperative store, said to Balagursamy one day, 'I have to give you some money. Please come to the store.'

When Balagurusamy went to the store, Prof. Velliyangiri said, 'Your notes have been sold for one thousand rupees. As royalty for that, we are paying you rupees one hundred at the rate of 10 per cent of the sale.' Balagurusamy was thrilled.

That was the first payment he received for preparing a textbook! The first royalty!

Knowing about the popularity of the notes, Khanna Publishers from Delhi approached Balagurusamy with a proposal to publish the notes as a book so that students from the entire country could benefit from it. Balagurusamy met the principal, Prof. Subbayyan, seeking his permission to publish it. Though Prof. Subbayyan held Balagurusamy in great regard, he refused permission to publish the book.

'I have so many years of experience in teaching. But I have not published any book so far. Why are you in a hurry to publish a book at so young an age?' he asked him.

'It is not my desire, sir,' Balagurusamy explained. 'The publishing company has approached me with the proposal.'

Prof. Subbayan did not relent. He refused to permit Balagurusamy to publish the book. Balagurusamy was disappointed and sad. But fate must have decided then that more than fifty internationally popular books would be published by Balagurusamy later on.

However, while he was busy with all this work, Balagurusamy secretly treasured a desire to pursue higher studies.

A Teacher as a Friend

Students loved Prof. Balagurusamy's classes. He had an innate ability to simplify problematic subjects for the students. Many of his students later went on to take very high positions in public life. One of them, Dr S. Salivahanan, is now the vice-chancellor of Vel Tech University in Chennai.

'Most of the teachers handled the classes with a sense of authority over the students. But this was not the way with Prof. Balagurusamy. He used to take classes with care, treating us like friends. This made his students understand and conceptualize what they have learned. No one else could take classes like this. As he treated all subjects with a sense of humour, his classes were a pleasant experience for us,' says Dr Salivahanan.

Dr Salivahanan studied electronics and communication engineering at PSG College. He joined the college in 1972. Balagurusamy left the college the same year. He was in Balagurusamy's classes only for a few months. Still, it was an unforgettable experience. 'When I met Balagurusamy, who was teaching Telephony and Telegraphy in the college, he looked like a senior student of the college. As he was the hostel warden also, students would go to him to clear their doubts there, too,' he recalls.

Prof. G.R. Damodaran, who had retired as the principal of the college, continued to render his services there as the correspondent and office bearer of the managing committee. He often came to the hostel to hold discussions with the wardens and students on the many things connected to the running of the hostel. He would listen to the students' opinions, suggestions and complaints and issue immediate orders. Once, Prof. Damodaran started talking with Balagurusamy after these official discussions had ended.

'What are your plans for the future?' he asked Balagurusamy.

The hope of a better tomorrow seemed to sprout in Balagurusamy's mind even as he heard the question.

'I want to become a teacher in the engineering college, Sir,' Balagurusamy replied.

'You must have a postgraduate degree in engineering for that, Balaguru,' Damodaran reminded him.

'Yes, Sir. It is my dream to get such a degree from one of the IITs,' Balagurusamy said.

'It is too late for that this year. This is July. Admissions to IITs close in June. And you have to qualify in the All India Entrance Examination to get admitted to IITs.'

Balagurusamy's face fell upon hearing this and Prof. Damodaran noted it.

'Come to my office tomorrow,' Prof. Damodaran instructed Balagurusamy.

Rays of hope again sparkled in Balagurusamy's mind!

10
A New World to Conquer

*The will to do achieves the deed
when the mind that wills is strong indeed.*

—Thirukkural 666

As instructed, Balagurusamy went to Prof. G.R. Damodaran's office the next day. Prof. Damodaran gave him a letter and said, 'Meet Dr Jai Krishna, the vice-chancellor of Roorkee University, and hand over this letter. He will do the needful for you to study for your ME there.'

Balagurusamy's joy knew no bounds.

He was also allowed a leave of absence for two years from PSG College. This was a special privilege which no one else had got before. Balagurusamy came to know from Prof. Narayanasamy and Prof. Lakshmanan, secretaries to Prof. G.R. Damodaran that Roorkee University was a world-renowned educational institution and ranked above the IITs.

With great enthusiasm, Balagurusamy got ready to go to Roorkee, a small town situated near the Himalayas. This was the first chance he got to go out of Tamil Nadu. Balagurusamy reached Delhi by the GT Express; from there, he had to travel more than 200 kilometres by bus to reach Roorkee. He met with difficulties in Delhi as he was not proficient in Hindi. Unless you know Hindi, it is difficult to even get a cup of tea there. Balagurusamy thought of the anti-Hindi agitation in which he had played a leading part while he was a student at the PSG Polytechnic. Now he realized the advantage one had of knowing one more language.

On reaching Roorkee he had to hire a cycle-rickshaw to go to the university. Balagurusamy felt that he could hold his own with the rickshaw puller with the broken Hindi he had at his command. He asked the fare before they even set off. The man said 'dedh rupya' (one and a half rupees). Balagurusamy felt that it was too much and said he would give only 'dhai rupya' (two and a half rupees). The rickshaw puller started laughing on hearing this. Balagurusamy had expected him to protest. When they reached the university, Balagurusamy paid him two and a half rupees, and the man gave one rupee back to him. It was only then that Balagurusamy realized his mistake. Even as he was walking down the courtyard of the university, he could not forget his embarrassment at the blunder he had committed.

The Honesty of the Poor

We constantly hear about taxi drivers and autorickshaw drivers who cheat passengers who come from other states and are not familiar with the local language. Balagurusamy always remembered the honesty of the poor rickshaw puller at Roorkee who gave him one rupee back when he was confused about the right word for the amount he had asked for as the fare. This incident played a significant role in forming his philosophy of life. How much better our society would be if no one wanted to amass wealth! Is there an end to the malady of gathering riches through corrupt practices?

The vice-chancellor of Roorkee University, Prof. Jai Krishna, had been a professor in the civil engineering department there for a long time. In those days, whenever there was an earthquake in any part of the world, Prof. Jai Krishna, nicknamed the 'Earthquake Expert', would be consulted by the authorities.

When Balagurusamy sought an appointment to meet the vice-chancellor, it was denied. But when he revealed that he had come with a letter from Prof. G.R. Damodaran and that it could be handed over only to the vice-chancellor, he was allowed in.

'There is an all-India examination for selecting students for the PG courses. Those selected at this preliminary examination have to take another test before they are selected. Now it is too late as the process has already been initiated for this year,' the vice-chancellor explained to Balagurusamy after reading the letter.

Prof. T.S. Madhava Rao, Head of the department of electrical engineering, was also present in the room when the vice-chancellor said this to Balagurusamy. However, Prof. Jai Krishna asked Prof. Madhava Rao if there was any chance of giving admission to this student.

'All the arrangements have been made. The test for the final selection is fixed for the coming Sunday,' he replied.

'Allow this candidate to appear for the examination as a special case,' Prof. Jai Krishna said.

Balagurusamy was surprised and he wondered how powerful the letter from Prof. Damodaran was.

It was Thursday. Balagurusamy stayed there for two days and appeared for the test on Sunday. After writing the test, he was not sure whether he would get admission there as many top achievers with BE degrees from all over the country had applied at Roorkee. He came to Delhi and decided to take the GT Express to go back home.

At the railway station, he met Ramamoorthy from Andhra Pradesh who too had taken the test. He, too, was not confident about the results of the test. They were not sure if they would ever come back to Delhi again. This thought made them decide that they should at least visit the Taj Mahal before going back. They could get down at Agra and continue their journey to the south on the next train. As they had regular train tickets without any reserved seats, it was possible to do so.

They got down at Agra and went around the magnificent edifice. Both of them were happy that they had taken this decision; however much you may read about it or see pictures of the beautiful structure, nothing equals the thrill of seeing the beauty with one's own eyes.

After he reached Coimbatore, with the beauty of one of the greatest wonders in the world still fresh in his mind, an even greater wonder awaited him. A telegram informed him that he had been selected for admission to the ME programme at Roorkee University.

Was he being lifted to the sky, or was the sky descending to touch him? He was not sure how to express his elation.

11
Self-confidence

No shame there is in poverty
For one (who is) strong, and of good quality.

—Thirukkural 988

Roorkee is a small town in the district of Haridwar in the state of Uttarakhand, which was previously in the state of Uttar Pradesh. The world-famous Roorkee University is ranked even higher than IITs. Only students who score high marks in the national entrance examination conducted by the university can get admission there. Scholarships are awarded depending on the performance of the students. Balagurusamy depended solely on the scholarship.

Soon after the beginning of the academic year, the weather changed, and it grew extremely cold. The ink in his pen was often frozen when he tried to write. Balagurusamy did not have any woollen clothes or other warm gear to protect himself from the biting cold. But there was one source of energy that drove him even in the most trying circumstances: study, study and study!

He had to face the first-semester examination of the university, braving the extreme cold climate of December. He passed the examination with a first class and even came first among all the students at the PG courses in the university. This gave his self-confidence a Himalayan boost.

At Roorkee, it was customary to include the students who had been placed first in the examinations in the University Consultative Council, University Students Council and University Students' Executive Council. As the best student, Balagurusamy became a member of all the three councils and was also chosen as the department leader. But he was not too keen on all these responsibilities. He had only one aim and that was to study well!

The students were not allowed to dress as they pleased, even in the hostels. The students, and those who worked there, had to wear formal clothes when they went to the dining hall. They had to address each other by their proper names, and everybody had to use a fork and spoon to eat at the dining table.

The hostel for postgraduate students was divided into two sections. The first-year students were in Azad Bhavan, named after the first minister for education in the government of India. Second-year students stayed in Nehru Bhavan, named after the first prime minister of independent India. Balagurusamy still considers himself lucky to have got a chance to stay in hostels named after such stalwarts.

Two years flew past quickly. Balagurusamy was intent on his sole aim of finishing the course with distinction. He won three gold medals at the end of the course, the Chancellor's Best Graduate Student Award of the University of Roorkee for 1972-74, Mukhopadhyaya Medal for the Best PG Student of the electrical engineering department of the university and a gold medal for obtaining the highest marks in ME (Electrical Engineering 1974), thus becoming the object of admiration of both students and faculty.

It was custom at Roorkee University to offer lecturership positions to those who secured the first rank among all the PG courses in the university. Balagurusamy could have got that position as he had come out on top of others. But he was not interested in it. He felt that he should go back to PSG, because the college had allowed him to take a 'leave of absence' for two years to complete the master's course.

So in May 1974, Balagurusamy started back for Coimbatore with an ME (Hons) degree. He was excited. His hard work was finally paying off and his dreams, it seemed, were gradually taking the shape of reality.

Since Balagurusamy had obtained a master's degree in engineering, he wanted to join the PSG Engineering College, leaving the PSG Polytechnic where he had been working before. He spoke directly to the principal, Prof. Subbayyan, about his desire.

'Since ours is an aided college, there are certain formalities prescribed by the government to be followed to appoint someone as a lecturer in the engineering college. A notification inviting applications will appear in the newspapers. You have to put in your application then,' said Prof. Subbayyan. As Prof. Subbayyan had explained, the process involved screening the applications of prospective candidates, and then inviting a few of them for an interview before taking the final decision on selection.

Balagurusamy was full of confidence as he submitted his application. He believed that his postgraduate degree from Roorkee University and his experience of teaching at PSG Polytechnic would enable him to get the post. He got the letter asking him to appear for an interview.

The interview board was headed by Prof. P. Sivalingam, director of technical education of Tamil Nadu, who later became the first vice-chancellor of Anna University. Others in the board were Prof. Subbayyan, principal of PSG College of Engineering; Dr A. Shanmugasundaram, head of the department of electrical engineering and Prof. S. Sampath, deputy director of IIT Madras. Prof. Sampath later became the director of IIT Kanpur, a member of the UPSC and the Scientific Advisor to Prime Minister Indira Gandhi. Dr Balagurusamy also served as a member of the UPSC later.

Prof. Sampath, who was leading the discussions, was very impressed by Balagurusamy's performance in Roorkee and his performance in the interview.

'Any more questions, gentlemen?' Prof. Sampath asked the other members of the board.

As nobody had anything more to ask, the interview was concluded. Prof. Sampath shook hands with Balagurusamy and wished him all the best, almost indicating that he had been selected. Balagurusamy left the room in joy.

But there was an unexpected turn of events. There was an obstacle in the path of Balagurusamy's appointment. Prof. Subbayyan informed the board that as some senior teachers in the civil and mechanical departments were awaiting promotions, it was impossible to appoint Balagurusamy.

Prof. Sampath then wanted to know what an appointment in the electrical department had to do with the civil and mechanical departments. When it became clear that the appointment would not be approved, Prof. Sampath understood that the interview had been a farce.

Expressing his disappointment at what had happened, he called Balagurusamy and said, 'Do not continue to work here any more. It will be of no use to you. Your ability will be recognized everywhere else. Don't waste your time here. Try to take a PhD from one of the IITs.'

Balagurusamy was saddened but the wisdom in the words of Prof. Sampath made a deep impression on him.

Prof. G.R. Damodaran had made it possible for him to go to Roorkee and complete his higher studies, but Balagurusamy did not inform Prof. Damodaran how his attempt to serve PSG College had been jeopardized by vested interests. He knew that the revelation would hurt Prof. Damodaran. At the same time, Balagurusamy knew that there was no point in remaining in Coimbatore any longer.

So the following day, before he went to his class at PSG, he handed his letter of resignation to the office of the head of the department. Prof. Shanmugasundaram, head of the department, sent for Balagurusamy as soon as the class was over. The letter was still in his hands.

'Why have you taken such a decision, Bala?' he asked.

'Sir, I am not interested in working here any more,' Balagurusamy replied.

'Why don't you reconsider?' the head of the department said.

'No, Sir, this is my decision,' Balagurusamy said firmly.

'All right, I will sign this. But you have to hand it over to the principal personally,' he said reluctantly, holding out the letter after he had affixed his signature. He must have thought that Balagurusamy might change his decision.

'No, Sir. As it has to be sent through the proper channels, I have handed in my resignation to you. Now I won't touch that letter. I won't meet the principal. You may forward it to the principal.'

Saying this, Balagurusamy left the room.

After resigning from his post at PSG Polytechnic, E. Balagurusamy was cautioned by a few of his colleagues and asked to reconsider his decision. However, despite the financial constraints, he had responded by saying that he would make a living by selling groundnuts in a pushcart

Farewell Party

It is customary to have a send-off meeting for those who leave their job in the college. His colleagues arranged such a meeting for Balagurusamy also. At first, he tried to avoid it. But when his close friend and colleague Prof. C.V. Roy took the lead in making all arrangements, he could not refuse to attend it. Roy had helped him a lot in preparing the notes on telephony and telegraphy in the form of a book. So he agreed to attend the farewell meeting on the condition that the principal, Prof. Subbayyan, should not be present at the meeting. In the end, the farewell meeting was held without inviting the principal.

Knowing that Balagurusamy would stand firm on his decision, Prof. Shanmugasundaram was forced to hand the resignation letter over to the principal. The principal, too, was not very happy at Balagurusamy leaving the institution.

'When Balagurusamy goes to the hostel, talk to him there and persuade him to reconsider,' the principal instructed Prof. Shanmugasundaram.

Prof. Shanmugasundaram knew that his attempt would not succeed. Still, he went to meet Balagurusamy at the hostel. He started talking in an amicable manner. 'Bala, you belong to a low-income family. If you throw away the job you have now, you will suffer a lot.'

'Sir, don't think that I am being impertinent. I have tendered my resignation, and it is my final decision. There is no change in that.' Balagurusamy did not show any hesitation while responding to Prof. Shanmugasundaram.

'Still, you have to live. How will you make a living?'

Prof. Shanmugasundaram made one more attempt.

'Sir, I will go around the Coimbatore-Avinashi Road, in front of this college, selling groundnuts in a pushcart with a signboard that says, "Balagurusamy, ME (Hons)". I will make more than a thousand rupees a month,' Balagurusamy thundered. He always believed in the dictum: Work is worship.

A lecturer was paid four hundred and fifty rupees a month in those days. Prof. Shanmugasundaram was shocked to hear what Balagurusamy said. He could say nothing further and left.

12

Aiming for the Sky

Let thoughts be always great and grand,
though they fail, their virtues stand.

—Thirukkural 596

In 1974, Balagurusamy returned to his village after leaving his job at the PSG College. While he remained at home for about a week, contemplating on his future, he found an advertisement in *The Hindu* inviting applications for research scholars in the IIT at Bombay. Balagurusamy remembered what Prof. Sampath had told him. So he sent an application to IIT Bombay. He also applied to the CSIR (Council of Scientific and Industrial Research) for its Senior Fellowship Programme under the Central Government. Within a few days, he received a call for an interview from IIT Bombay.

The interview board at IIT Bombay consisted of Prof. V. Subbarao, an expert in electrical machines; Prof. A.K. De, the director of IIT and Prof. G.N. Revankar, head of electrical engineering department and an expert in control systems. They were delighted to see the very high marks that Balagurusamy had scored in his master's degree from Roorkee University.

'What subject would you like to choose for your research, Balaguru?' asked Prof. Subbarao.

'I want to research reliability engineering,' said Balagurusamy.

'But there is no one here who has specialized in that subject to be your guide. Why don't you choose electrical machines? In that case, I can be your guide,' Prof. Subbarao said.

'Sorry, Sir. I am interested only in reliability engineering as the subject for my research. Please allow me to do that,' Balagurusamy said firmly.

The board was not entirely happy with the candidate's obstinacy, but he was allowed to have his way as they did not want to lose such a brilliant scholar. The list of selected candidates was published in the evening on the same day, and Balagurusamy was thrilled to see his name on the list.

The interview took place in July 1974, and he had to join on the 1st of August. Balagurusamy reached Bombay in the afternoon on 31 July. On his arrival at Bombay Matunga railway station, he was caught up in an agitation by the Shiv Sena and could not go any further. So he left his suitcase in the cloakroom in the Matunga railway station and searched for a place to stay the night. He got a bed in a room for two in a lodge nearby. He was happy with it as he only wanted a place to spend the night. A man was sleeping on one of the beds when Balagurusamy reached there. Balagurusamy lay down on the other bed and soon fell asleep.

When he woke up the following morning, the other man was gone, and so was the purse Balagurusamy had kept in the pocket of his trousers. When he complained to the lodge manager, the man did not even care to give a proper reply. Another man who was standing nearby said, 'This is common here. We have to be careful.'

Fortunately, Balagurusamy was in the habit of keeping his money in different places. He would keep an amount in the pocket of his trousers, some in his shirt and the rest in the purse. As he had already paid for the bed, he had just enough money to have something to eat for breakfast and travel to IIT located at Powai.

Setbacks had become a part of life for Balagurusamy and he could face situations like these with equanimity. He was calm even though he had lost almost all the money he had with him in a strange city. He travelled by electric train and walked the rest of the way, reaching IIT with just fifty paise left in his pocket.

He went to the office and told them about the loss of money. He was not able to pay the fees and wanted some time for that. The officer there told him, 'That is all right. You can join the course and the hostel. Don't worry about it. When you get your fellowship money, you can make the payment.'

Balagurusamy was relieved upon hearing this from the authorities.

They arranged for a room in the hostel and provisions for food as well. Balagurusamy could not even buy a sheet to spread on the wooden cot!

Balagurusamy met another research scholar from Tamil Nadu who had attended the interview with him. The scholar, Balasubramanian, had studied at IIT Kanpur before coming to Bombay. Balagurusamy told him about the loss of his purse with a faint hope that someone from his state would perhaps be ready to help him at such a critical time. But the man did not even respond to Balagurusamy appropriately. This made Balagurusamy feel sad. In any case, he bought an inland letter for ten paise and wrote to one of his friends at the PSG College, who then sent him a money order for four hundred rupees. After almost twenty days, he was able to buy some essential things and pay his fees. He took special care to see that no one knew about his financial restraints. He did not want anyone to think that he was trying to get help by talking about his difficulties.

Balagurusamy had a special place among the students as an alumna of the prestigious University of Roorkee. They were equally awed by the high marks he had scored. As there was nobody to be his guide in the subject he had chosen, Prof. De and Prof. Revankar came forward to be the joint guides, even though both of them had no previous research experience in the subject.

'Bala, you should prepare the reports on your research work yourself. We can only go through your reports and evaluate your work. We cannot guide you in your research,' said the guides. They were ready to reveal their helplessness. Such an unfavourable atmosphere only added to Balagurusamy's determination, and his guides had complete confidence in his ability.

Balagurusamy had also applied for a Senior Fellowship awarded by CSIR. CSIR awards Junior Fellowships to postgraduate students and Senior Fellowships to PhD students. Balagurusamy had indicated in the application that he desired to do his research at the University of Roorkee.

The letter informing him that he had been selected for the CSIR Fellowship reached Andipattikottai only after Balagurusamy had joined IIT Bombay, and it was redirected to the IIT hostel. His joy knew no bounds when he got the letter allowing him to do his research at the University of Roorkee.

Balagurusamy had heard that it would take a long time to finish his PhD at IIT Bombay. But as he had confidence in his ability and readiness to work hard, he thought he would submit his thesis within the minimum period of twenty-four months. Still, he approached Prof. Revankar for clarification. 'Sir, how long will it take for me to finish my research?' he asked.

'For most students, it takes a long time. But knowing your interest and ability, I think you will be able to complete it in four to five years,' replied Prof. Revankar.

'Sir, I thought I would be able to finish in two years,' Balagurusamy said.

'That is impossible. You have to continue your research work for at least four years,' Prof. Revankar said.

It was like asking someone who moved at the speed of a jet engine to take a bullock cart!

'Sir, I have got the CSIR fellowship to do my research at the University of Roorkee,' Balagurusamy informed him.

'Oh, very good! Then that should be the best choice for you. You continue your research at Roorkee,' Revankar said happily. He must have been relieved to have got out of being a guide on a subject that was unknown to him.

November 14, 1974, was Deepavali, the time when the celebration of lights turned night into day! Balagurusamy's mind, too, was filled with brightness and colours! He set out for Roorkee that night itself by Paschim Express.

He entered the University of Roorkee with the joy of one returning to his home. He knew that stalwarts like Prof. Krishna B. Mishra and Prof. Madhava Rao were there to guide him in his chosen field. Prof. Mishra had been the first to research into reliability engineering for his PhD. Balagurusamy approached Prof. Mishra with all the documents. Prof. Mishra had seen the project reports that Balagurusamy had submitted when he was doing his ME there. So he did not hesitate in accepting him as his student

Balagurusamy had to go to Coimbatore to get some papers from

PSG College. He went to meet Prof. G.R. Damodaran. He did not tell him how he had been disgraced at PSG College when he had wanted to work there. Prof. Damodaran was unhappy that Balagurusamy had left the college without informing him.

'You left without telling me anything, Bala,' Prof. Damodaran said.

'I do not want to make any complaints against anybody, Sir. That is why I had to leave without meeting you. You must pardon me for that,' Balagurusamy replied.

However, Prof. Damodaran was delighted to know that Balagurusamy had decided to go for his PhD. With his blessings and all the papers that were needed, Balagurusamy returned to Roorkee.

13

'I Stick to My Rights'

Elephants are firm when arrows hit.
Great minds keep fit even in defeat.

—Thirukkural 597

It was winter. Balagurusamy immersed himself in his chosen subject despite the bitter cold once he was accepted as a research scholar under Prof. K.B. Mishra. Recognizing the calibre of the scholar, Prof. Mishra arranged for a separate room and other facilities for Balagurusamy to have the support he needed. And the student rose to the occasion by completing his first research paper in forty-five days. The other scholars had not even decided upon the title for their paper by that time.

Balagurusamy tried to meet Prof. Mishra to get his paper published in *IEEE Transactions on Reliability*, a world-famous research journal. In the evening, he went to the professor's house and made his request. He had already sent the research paper to the professor.

Prof. Mishra went on to talk about various irrelevant things. But he did not come to the question of the paper's publication. It was getting late at night, and the temperature was freezing.

Balagurusamy sat there patiently, listening to him. In the end, he brought up the subject.

'Did you go through my paper, Sir?' Balagurusamy asked. Prof. Mishra handed him the paper he had sent him earlier. As Balagurusamy glanced through the article, he realized that Prof. Mishra had made no changes in the paper except for one on the first page. 'E. Balagurusamy and Prof. K.B. Mishra' had been changed to 'Prof. K.B. Mishra and E. Balagurusamy'.

It was customary to add the guide's name to the paper even though the work had been done by the scholar alone. Balagurusamy had not given much thought to that; he had included the name of his guide after his name as a matter of courtesy.

'You must excuse me, Sir, but I cannot accept this change. I included your name as a courtesy as you are my guide,' Balagurusamy said seriously.

All the professor's arguments did not make him change his decision.

He said, 'Sir, in that case, I am going back. I don't want any PhD.'

Mishra could not believe his ears! He did not want to lose such a promising young scholar.

'This paper is the result of my work. I am not prepared to share the credit for that with anyone,' saying this, Balagurusamy got up.

'Sit down, Bala. Oh! You Madrasis! You are all so short-tempered!' he said. People from the southern states of India were referred to as 'Madrasis' by those in the northern states.

Balagurusamy was shaking. But it was not anger that made him shiver; it was the extreme cold of winter.

'Don't you have a sweater?' Mishra asked.

'I don't have the money to buy one, Sir,' Balagurusamy revealed. Mishra called his wife and asked her to fetch a coat for Balagurusamy.

But Balagurusamy refused to accept it. After asking his wife to get some hot tea, the professor went on talking in a bid to make his student cool down. Then he put forth a suggestion. 'Put your name first in this paper, but it should be my name that comes first in the next one. This pattern can be repeated. What do you say?'

'Okay.' He agreed and with that one word the problem was solved. After that, Balagurusamy's name appeared first in seven papers he submitted, and Prof. Mishra's name was written first in seven others. Balagurusamy's papers kept appearing in world-famous publications—almost at the rate of one each month. In twelve months, he had published fourteen papers. 'Paper Printing Machine' was the nickname the campus honoured him with!

DEVELOPING FORTRAN PROGRAMS

As part of his research work, Balagurusamy developed a number of unique mathematical models for the estimation of reliability of different kinds of redundant systems. It was practically impossible to evaluate these models manually and study the reliability behaviour of these systems. Therefore, it became necessary to develop computer programs, execute them on suitable computers and then tabulate the results for further analysis.

During the 1970s, not many programming languages were available to evaluate mathematical models. The only available language was FORTRAN, which stands for formula translation. Balagurusamy learned FORTRAN programming on his own and developed programs using the language. These programs had to be punched on cards specially designed for this purpose. These punched cards had to then be fed into a computer that supported the FORTAN language. The computer would read the data in the punched cards, process it and provide the results as output.

As Roorkee University did not have a suitable computer at that time, Balagurusamy had to go to the Structural Engineering Research Centre (SERC) located nearby. SERC had an IBM1620 computer, a reasonably fast one for its time, and Roorkee University students were permitted to use SERC's computing facilities. Balagurusamy used to spend many evenings and nights there, developing programs, debugging them and executing them on the IBM1620 computer. Thus, Balagurusamy became an expert in computer programming as early as 1975.

HONOURS ARE NOT TO BE SHARED

At the end of each academic year, the Khosla Research Award, in honour of the former vice-chancellor of the University of Roorkee, is presented for the best research work that year. The award consists of a certificate and a gold medal.

When the research report was prepared for submission for the award, Prof. Mishra pleaded, 'My name must come first, at least in this report, Bala.'

Balagurusamy obliged readily. Balagurusamy was delighted to know that their report had been selected for the Khosla Research Award that year. But Balagurusamy was shocked when he read the award letter. 'Prof. Mishra will receive the gold medal, and Balagurusamy will receive the certificate!'

Balagurusamy was not one to suffer such injustice in silence.

'I am not interested in getting a PhD degree, Sir; I am going home,' Balagurusamy said again, confronting Prof. Mishra with the letter informing him of the award in hand. 'I fail to find any trace of justice in this. I do all the hard work, and you get the gold medal.' Balagurusamy was furious.

At first, Prof. Mishra tried to ignore him, but in the end, he had to give in and write to the vice-chancellor of the University of Roorkee saying that the gold medal too should go to Balagurusamy. That gold medal was surely worth more than its weight in gold!

Fourteen months after joining the course, Balagurusamy was ready to submit his research thesis, including all the reports that he had published. He approached Prof. Mishra to submit his thesis to the university.

'As per the rules, you have to complete two years as a research scholar. You can submit the thesis only after that,' Prof. Mishra said and held steadfast to his decision.

Balagurusamy could not agree. He wrote to the vice-chancellor directly, giving the details of all the research papers and the thesis report that he had prepared. The vice-chancellor, after careful consideration, realized that Balagurusamy had completed all the requirements to be awarded a PhD degree in terms of research work. But he could not take a decision on such a matter all by himself. So he ordered the constitution of a three-member expert committee to consider Balagurusamy's claim. The committee took two months to go through the thesis and the papers in detail and then announced its decision.

'Balagurusamy's research papers and thesis are much better than what is generally expected from a research scholar, and so he may be permitted to submit his thesis for the PhD degree. We are treating it as a special case,' said the expert committee report.

Balagurusamy thus came to hold the distinction of being the first to submit the PhD thesis in the shortest period at Roorkee University.

Bridegroom Wanted!

There were many central government organizations in Rourkee, such as the Central Building Research Institute (CBRI), SERC and a large base of defence establishments, besides Roorkee University. Many Tamil Brahmins held important positions in these organizations. Balagurusamy became famous among the people from Tamil Nadu in Roorkee as the most brilliant young research scholar in engineering at the University of Roorkee. The other students from Tamil Nadu already held him to be their undisputed leader. These students used to take part in all the major Tamil festivities of that place, thereby adding to the prestige of the Tamil families there.

Many of the Brahmins thought that Balagurusamy belonged to their caste. So they used to invite him to eat with them on important occasions. Balagurusamy never refused these invitations. It was customary to introduce the guest to all the members of the family. They were very particular in introducing their daughters. Some of them wanted to see if Balagurusamy's horoscope matched those of their daughters in an attempt to get him as their son-in-law.

When he realized what was being planned, he tactfully avoided appearing at their houses for celebrations.

14
A Strong Sense of Direction

*A powerful mind does a powerful act,
and all the rest are imperfect.*

—Thirukkural 661

The desire to visit his village grew strong in Balagurusamy's mind once he had finished his PhD. Upon his return, the pristine nature and the pure air did much to bring calm and happiness to his mind.

While staying in the village, he knew that Bharat Heavy Electricals Limited (BHEL) was recruiting engineers. He sent an application outlining his educational qualification, experience and all other relevant details, along with a cover letter to V. Krishnamurthy, chairman and managing director of BHEL in New Delhi.

BHEL earlier had independent establishments at nine places, including Delhi, Bhopal, Haridwar, Trichy, Hyderabad and Jhansi, each manufacturing one type of electrical equipment. In 1974, Prime Minister Indira Gandhi brought all the establishments under one unit for better administrative control; the merged unit was named Bharat Heavy Electricals Limited and Krishnamurthy became its founder, chairman and managing director. He was well known as a great techno-administrator and popularly called the 'Father of the Public Sector in India'.

Balagurusamy was interviewed by Krishnamurthy and selected for appointment as research engineer in October 1976. He was posted to the Energy Systems and New Products (ESNP) division of BHEL in New Delhi. Karan, who hailed from Bihar, worked as the Assistant General Manager of the ESNP division. When he went through Balagurusamy's bio-data, he was amazed. Only a few engineers in the division had got their master's degree. There were only one or two who had a PhD to their credit. Karan was responsible for allotting work to the engineers under him. Balagurusamy was the only one among them who had specialized in reliability engineering. Karan himself had little knowledge about the subject, even though he was the Assistant General Manager. Realizing the qualification and potential of the young engineer under him, he said to Balagurusamy, 'You will have the freedom to take any decision and put it into practice on matters related to research and development.'

Recognition of his capability boosted Balagurusamy's morale to a very high level. Though he had changed from teaching to research, he did not find it difficult to immerse himself in the work.

Balagurusamy undertook a detailed study of various developmental projects essential for BHEL. He approached Karan with a proposal to develop computer software for the analysis of failure of boiler tubes in different thermal plants across the country. The large-hearted superior was quite frank. 'Bala, I do not know this subject. You take the decision and do whatever is needed.'

BHEL had been supplying boiler tubes to almost all the thermal power stations in the country. These boiler tubes failed very often, and when they needed some repairs, it was necessary to stop production of electricity. Balagurusamy wanted to develop new software that would help them find the reason for the frequent breakdown of the pipes and also how to prevent it. As the first step, Balagurusamy developed a computer program that explained how the boiler tubes got damaged. The program, named 'Performance Analysis of Boiler Plants', was created using the computer language FORTAN-IV.

A national Emergency was declared on 25 June 1975. Balagurusamy could not find a house or even a room to stay in Delhi. He had to stay for many months at BHEL's guest house. House owners back then were not ready to rent their houses to bachelors. After a long search, he managed to rent a part of the house of a Punjabi gentleman working in a bank in Lajpat Nagar. This man was also reluctant to allow a bachelor to stay on the first floor while he was himself occupying the ground floor. But Balagurusamy had become wiser about the ways of the world and showed him his visiting card, which proclaimed, 'Dr E. Balagurusamy, ME (Hons), PhD', and informed him that he was working in BHEL. He also told the Punjabi that he was to get married in three to four months, and after that, his wife would be staying with him. The man was quite impressed, and he allowed Balagurusamy to stay there.

Balagurusamy had not received any proposals of marriage at that time. Each month, the house owner would enquire about his marriage, and Balagurusamy would find one excuse after the other. He even told him, 'I will soon bring my wedding card and invite you to the function. You must come for that.'

During the Emergency, punctuality became a 'mantra' at all places. At BHEL, work started at 7.45 a.m. Everybody would be on time. When the employees signed the attendance register kept at the entrance to the office, they had to enter the time shown on the clock there. The company even had a strict procedure for the employees to get into the company buses. All this punctuality and strict obedience to rules was necessary because of the Emergency. 'If only our people were ready to follow the rules and be punctual at all times, our country would have progressed so fast,' laments Balagurusamy often.

The emergency was lifted in March 1977 and general elections were announced. A.B. Vajpayee was to contest from the Delhi South constituency, where Lajpat Nagar was included. Balagurusamy had already met Vajpayee at Roorkee as his nephew was Balagurusamy's classmate in the ME class. The eminent personality had attracted him. Vajpayee had fired the imagination of the youth with his poetic and oratorical skills. Out of mere eagerness, Balagurusamy and his friends campaigned for Vajpayee in South Delhi.

The Essence of Simplicity

Dr V. Krishnamurthy, former chairman of BHEL, is in his nineties now. When asked about Balagurusamy, he replied with a happy smile. 'Balaguru entered BHEL after he had finished his PhD in reliability engineering at Roorkee. I was his boss then. There were many who were very good at engineering there. But only very few could keep up with the new technologies that were being developed. I saw that Balaguru was competent at keeping abreast of developing technology.

In the Energy Division of BHEL, we had projects to develop new products in solar and other non-conventional energy systems. I saw that only Balaguru could study all that in detail and then put them into practical use. But unfortunately, that brilliant young man was with us only for two years. I, too, left the organisation soon. Though I did not meet him for a long time after that, through the media, I followed his successes and saw the good he did in all the areas he touched.

He put up a brilliant show as the technical consultant for the government of Andhra Pradesh. I was there as the advisor to the Chief Minister N.T. Ramarao and I witnessed the dedication with which Balaguru implemented the computer-based projects in the government departments of Andhra Pradesh. Then he became the vice-chancellor of Anna University. It was indeed a great responsibility.

It is not an easy job to be in charge of over 250 engineering colleges and other colleges under the university. Balaguru tried his best to improve the standard of all the colleges under the university while he was the vice-chancellor. He was always concerned about the welfare of students and teachers.

I was able to keep up my friendship with Balagurusamy when I went to Anna University to meet Dr Kalam, who was the emeritus professor there. When the central government wanted to make Dr Balagurusamy a member of the Union Public Service Commission, Prime Minister Dr Manmohan Singh had asked me about him. I informed the Prime Minister that it would be difficult to find another person as brilliant as Balaguru, and that he was deeply knowledgable in scientific subjects. More than all that, I told Mr Singh that he was the essence of simplicity and honesty to the core.'

Dr Krishnamurthy feels that the Tamil Nadu government did not make full use of the brilliance of Balagurusamy.

(While the final work on this book was going on Krishnamurthy passed away at Chennai on 29 June 2022.)

At that time, there was a rumour doing the rounds at BHEL that Balagurusamy was a close relative of Krishnamurthy, the chairman of BHEL. Although Krishnamurthy was his boss, Balagurusamy had never met Krishnamurthy in person after joining BHEL. But Balagurusamy was not in the habit of listening to gossip, and he went on with his work undisturbed. But after some time, he felt irritated by this baseless fiction. He was happy with the work he was doing, even though it was not equivalent to his qualifications. Still, he never showed any disappointment or displeasure in his career.

At this juncture, Balagurusamy had occasion to meet Prof. Y. Saran, the principal of the Technical Teachers' Training Institute (TTTI) at Bhopal in Madhya Pradesh. They had detailed discussions about Balagurusamy's background and interests. Within a month, Balagurusamy got a letter asking him to appear for an interview for the post of an assistant professor at the institute. A second-class train ticket was also enclosed. BHEL had allowed the candidates to travel first class when they came for the interview. Balagurusamy felt disappointed and sent a reply saying that he was not interested in travelling by second class. Soon afterwards, Balagurusamy got a letter from Prof. Saran saying that he was coming to Delhi to participate in the meeting of the National Council of Educational Research and Training (NCERT) and he expressed his desire to meet Balagurusamy in person.

Prof. Saran was a close friend of Prof. G.R. Damodaran, Correspondent of the PSG Trust at Coimbatore. The Government of India had appointed a high-power committee in 1969 to revamp polytechnic education in the country, with Prof. Damodaran as the chairman and Prof. Saran as member secretary. It was popularly known as the Damodaran Committee. That was how Prof. Damodaran and Prof. Saran had become closely associated. From Prof. Damodaran, Prof. Saran had heard about Balagurusamy. He, therefore, knew that though he was brilliant, Balagurusamy was not very tolerant. Prof. Saran did not want to lose such an intelligent man like Balagurusamy and decided to meet him in person despite the letter of rejection he had received.

'It is tough to find people with such academic qualifications as you have. We would like you to join TTTI,' said Prof. Saran. The chairman of the TTTI Management Board, who was also present, expressed the same view. Balagurusamy was elated at the thought of going back to his favourite teaching profession. And here, he would be teaching the faculty of polytechnics and engineering colleges in the country. That was an important assignment. He did not think twice before giving up the job at BHEL.

On the 1st of April 1977, Balagurusamy left for Bhopal, where a life of varied experiences awaited him.

Change of Status of TTTI

The central government established TTTIs in four regions of India. The institute for the southern region was at Tharamani in Chennai. The others were at Bhopal, Chandigarh and Kolkata. Prof. Y. Saran was the director of the institute at Bhopal.

The TTTI aimed at offering continuing education and training programmes for the faculty of the technical institutions, developing need-based curricula and instructional material, and undertaking research and development in technical education. The TTTI was upgraded in 2003 as the National Institute of Technical Teachers' Training and Research (NITTTR).

15

New Avenues

Water's depth is lotus-height,
mental strength is men's merit.

—Thirukkural 595

Bhopal is popularly known as the 'city of lakes'. There are many natural and artificial lakes that add to the beauty of the green city. Balagurusamy had passed through hurricanes and thunderstorms of bad experiences so far in his life. Here, life seemed to offer something pleasant, like a fragrant gentle breeze. The cooperative nature of his colleagues there enabled him to begin a new chapter in his life.

While he was teaching at the TTTI and staying at the hostel attached to it for about four months, he got a letter from Prof. K.B. Mishra, who had been his PhD guide at Roorkee.

'Dear Bala,' the letter read. 'I have been approached by the publisher McGraw Hill Education, New Delhi to write a book on reliability engineering. The research papers that you have written on reliability are very good and incomparable. Why don't we both co-write the book for McGraw-Hill?'

It is a matter of immense pride for a student to have his former teacher ask him whether they both could produce a book together. Here it was the world-famous McGraw Hill that was asking to publish it. As Balagurusamy had written every word of the papers on reliability engineering for his research, the professor knew that only Balagurusamy would be able to describe the concepts in simple language. That must have prompted him to write the letter to Balagurusamy. Balagurusamy readily agreed to his suggestion.

Ask for a flower and be gifted a garden

While working as an instructor at the PSG Polytechnic in 1965, Balagurusamy had wanted to be enrolled for training at the TTTI in Chennai. He felt that he would be able to take classes for the students in a better way if he got that training and so he applied for admission there. With the high marks and the qualification he possessed, he was selected. Those who had been selected needed to be sponsored by the institution in which they were working. Balagurusamy approached the college authorities for support. But they refused to oblige him. He was asked to resign from the job and go for training if he wanted. So he had to give up a chance to be trained at the TTTI. But twelve years later, Dr Balagurusamy entered the portals of the TTTI as a trainer for the teachers of engineering colleges. A fitting tribute to his ability and hard work!

He wrote to his former guide, 'Sir, I am thrilled to be a part of this work. I have divided the subject of reliability engineering into fourteen chapters and added more details to make it easy for the students to understand the subject. Each chapter has been again divided into different topics for the same purpose. You may prepare the material for any seven chapters, and I will do the same for the rest of them. Please let me know your choice of chapters.' Balagurusamy posted the details to Prof. Mishra.

Balagurusamy waited in vain for more than six months for a response from Prof. Mishra. Then he wrote to McGraw Hill saying that he had published many papers in international journals on reliability engineering and expressed his willingness to put them together in the form of a textbook. McGraw Hill accepted Balagurusamy's offer. Balagurusamy used the papers he had published for the book and added more details that he had come upon while working as a teacher. He could add all the latest information on the subject in the book.

When someone was using the material published as research papers for making a book, it was necessary to get the permission of the university. So Balagurusamy wrote to the registrar of the University of Roorkee and obtained the consent.

No other book on reliability engineering had so far been published in India. Hence Balagurusamy was determined to make his book easy enough for students to understand the subject. Within seven months of his starting to work on the book, he was able to complete it, giving a comprehensive analysis of the subject. The publishers also were determined to make sure that the book they brought out was the best in the world. So they sent Balagurusamy's manuscript to three eminent people researching on the subject for their opinion. It took some time for them to go through the work. In the end, they informed the publishers of their opinion after a deep and detailed study. All three of them were unanimous in expressing their opinion that the contents were of a very high standard. They were happy that such a book was being published in India. Balagurusamy included the explanations that he had given for the questions of these three people also in the book. Thus, the first book written by Balagurusamy was published in 1984. It was also the first book by an Indian author on reliability engineering.

Though he could claim credit for the entire work, Balagurusamy did not forget the support and encouragement provided by his guide, Prof. K.B. Mishra, both directly and indirectly. As a token of respect to his guru, he dedicated the book to Prof. K.B. Mishra. This book on reliability engineering authored by Balagurusamy was prescribed as the textbook for MTech students in IITs and universities in the 1980s and 1990s. Prof. K.B. Mishra was happy and proud that a book written by one of his research students had been prescribed as a text for students of IITs.

GURUDAKSHINA

When he heard that the biography of Dr Balagurusamy was being written, Prof. K.B. Mishra tried to recollect their relationship more than thirty years ago. Though he could not remember everything clearly, he could confidently assert with pride that Balagurusamy was a scholar of the highest calibre.

'I have acted as a guide for forty-three research scholars who took their PhD under me. But I cannot think of another student with as much intelligence and ability as Balagurusamy. At that time, the Government of India had not earmarked any funds for research in reliability engineering. But we would not have been able to compete with countries like Japan and America without doing theoretical research on reliability. So I decided to undertake research independently, without anybody to guide me, and earned my PhD. Later I gave shape to the 'Graph Theory to System Reliability Evaluation'. That had a remarkable impact. That helped me approach reliability through engineering. I persuaded Balagurusamy to continue his research on that subject. I remember with pride the outstanding achievements that Balagurusamy made in the field. He aims at perfection in any work that he undertakes. His dedication and hard work will amaze anyone. He has prepared numerous research papers and published them in prestigious international journals like *IEEE Transactions on Reliability* and *Microelectronics Reliability*. This was a trait not generally seen in research scholars. Balagurusamy was the only student who finished his research project way ahead of time and got his doctorate. In 1984, Balagurusamy sent me a copy of the first book that he had published. It was only when I opened the book that I realized that Balagurusamy had dedicated the book to me as 'gurudakshina' (a gift offered to the preceptor by the student at the end of his education). I wrote to him to express my gratitude.

'I realized how calm and level-headed he used to be as a student, how curious he was as a research scholar, and more than all that, how warm-hearted and loving he was as a human being. Unlike other scholars who dressed up in suits and coats, Balagurusamy used to wear simple clothes, even during the winter.

'While he was working in Delhi, he took me to the place where he was staying. It was just a tiny room with only a cot in it. That night, he made me sleep on the bed, and he curled up on the floor with a bed sheet. I can never forget the care and devotion that he extended to me that day, even keeping the heater near me to keep me warm.'

16
Spring Comes

*What is rare when wife is good,
what can be there when she is wrong?*

—Thirukkural 53

Balagurusamy was happy with the work that he was doing in Bhopal. He enjoyed discussing academic as well as non-academic matters with his student trainees. He continued this habit even when he was the vice-chancellor of Anna University. He was interested in making his students aware of the latest information in their field of study. He kept himself alert and when he came to know about students' financial difficulties, he would offer them whatever help he could. This humane interest in the welfare of his students later made him act stringently against those colleges that were adopting practices that were causing difficulties for the students.

Prof. K.B. Mishra was his supervisor during his research, and he played a significant role in bringing out the first book that Balagurusamy ever wrote. But there was another person by his side who offered him support and helped him bring out many books later in his life. That person was also working in the TTTI at Bhopal, a lady—one who could transform the storms that raged in his mind into a soothing breeze of peace and quiet. Sushila had a doctorate in management and worked in the TTTI at Bhopal. Balagurusamy saw her as a good colleague.

At that time, Balagurusamy's family was persuading him to get married to a girl they had chosen for him from their clan. When this pressure became too much of a bother, Balagurusamy even decided not to get married to avoid a relationship that he was not very keen on.

For someone who had accepted teaching almost like a penance, where was the chance to think of married life? But as time passed, Balagurusamy found that his colleague Sushila's tastes, thoughts and attitudes, seemed to flow smoothly along with his own. Thus, she found a place in his mind on a level higher than that of just a colleague.

Mental Harmony

Let us hear what Dr Hemalatha, who retired as a professor of mathematics from Anna University has to say. 'Balagurusamy and Sushila, who were teachers at the TTTI, Bhopal, were two people who shared the same thoughts and worked along the same path of action. Sushila madam was the most suitable person to share the life of someone like Balagurusamy. Both of them were full of compassion. They were both honest to the core. They would be in the lead in any matter that would bring good to (the) society in general. They never interfered in other people's affairs. Balagurusamy and Sushila would never hesitate to help, comfort and provide mental support to anyone going through difficult times. Social responsibility and compassion were what stood out in their characters and both of them loved teaching. The two of them were courteous towards their guests and would extend a warm welcome to those who came to meet them. In short, they were really 'made for each other' in all senses of the saying.'

There was nothing of the usual youthful romance developing between them. High social values, as well as ideals of academic excellence, filled their minds. It could not be described as a 'love affair' in any sense of the term; more that they shared similar ideas and ideals.

At that time, there were only two women working in the TTTI. One of them was Sushila, and the other was Manjul Saxena. Manjul Saxena was a professor there, while Sushila was an assistant professor. They were very close to each other. It was Manjul who was instrumental in bringing Sushila and Balagurusamy together.

Balagurusamy and Sushila had travelled to many parts of the

country to participate in discussions and seminars representing the TTTI. This gave them a chance to get to know each other better. It was Manjul Saxena who first realized that if Balagurusamy and Sushila started living together, they could be the most ideal couple. She took the initiative and sat down with both of them to talk about it. The next steps were taken quickly.

Both of them were least interested in rituals and celebrations, and both were against wasting a working day. So they decided to get married on a public holiday. On 26 January 1981, Balagurusamy and Sushila got married in a simple ceremony that lasted for half an hour, 5.30 p.m. to 6 p.m., at the Arya Samaj in Bhopal.

Balagurusamy was 35 and Sushila 33 at that time. Prof. Mani, the principal of TTTI, and his wife stood as legal guardians for Balagurusamy, while Manjul Saxena and her husband did the same for Sushila.

Relatives of the bride and the groom could not attend the function due to the distance from their native places and the lack of time, both acting as hurdles for making arrangements for the journey. The fact that Balagurusamy had refused to marry the girl of their choice also must have stopped his family from coming to Bhopal for the ceremony.

His neighbours in the TTTI staff quarters were shocked when they saw Balagurusamy arriving home with his wife! All his friends and colleagues were present at the reception that Balagurusamy arranged at the college guest house the following evening.

Both of them were back at work the very next day. Their honeymoon was spent at work in the institution. Balagurusamy had avoided taking leave throughout his life—both when he was studying and working. Even when he was learning to read and write at the school held on the verandah of one of the houses at Andipattikottai, Balagurusamy would be present there even on holidays.

After marriage, Balagurusamy became very close to Sushila's family in Rajkot. They, too, held their 'Jeejaji' in great respect and affection. Balagurusamy used to visit them regularly until he became a UPSC Member.

Sushila was very devout and liked to visit different temples and make offerings. Balagurusamy was not interested in such affairs. Despite a few such differences, they lived happily without any significant differences of opinion. 'My wife used to visit temples regularly. Sometimes she would say, "I want to worship at Tirupati Temple and offer some money in the hundi. I need fifty thousand rupees." I would give her the amount, even though I was not in favour of this habit of putting money in the hundi. We may have had some slight difference of opinion on such matters. But we both shared the same values concerning a sense of responsibility, charity and compassion, and used to participate in activities related to these with enthusiasm. This enabled us to lead a happy and contented life with mutual respect.' These words reveal Dr Balagurusamy's attitude towards companionship and life.

17

Fragrance for the Flower

Wisdom checks the straying senses
Expels evils, impels goodness

—Thirukkural 422

At the principal's office at St. Xavier's College, Ahmedabad, a young woman who was also a lecturer working there entered the office like a gentle breeze. She left like a raging tornado. She had come to ask for a leave of absence for three days. She had the leave letter, which she held out and made the request respectfully. Her pleasant demeanour and spirited nature could attract the attention of all who saw her.

'No, I can't grant you any leave. We have to conduct tests for the students here,' the principal said sternly.

'I had already informed you when I joined here that I have to appear for an examination to go for higher studies. You had promised to do what was necessary when the time came. Is it right to say that you can't sanction my leave now?' the young lady reminded the principal.

'Your request for leave is for a purely personal matter. Here we have to conduct tests for the students. You, too, have a responsibility. Which is more important, your matter or something that affects your students?' The principal was not ready to reconsider the decision.

'Isn't this a class test? It can be held under the supervision of any of the teachers here. I have completed all the work I have to do in connection with the tests. If I do not write this examination now, my chances of higher studies will be jeopardized. Please don't do this,' she spoke clearly in a firm tone.

'I don't want to hear any explanations from you. I will not sanction your leave,' the principal spoke as if it were the last words.

'...Then I will resign,' the answer came immediately. Her firm words shocked the principal. She immediately submitted her resignation letter and left the room like a whirlwind. The young lady who threw her job away rather than compromise her self-respect was Prof. Sushila, who later became the wife of Dr Balagurusamy.

Kannadasan, a famous lyricist of Tamil Nadu, has said, 'Getting a good wife is the greatest blessing of God.' As Sushila and Balagurusamy became life partners, they transformed into a model couple, one complementing the other like gold and its sheen, like flowers and their fragrance.

Sushila was born to a middle-class family in Gujarat in 1948. Her father, Narsian, an advocate, passed away when she was still a small girl. So her mother brought up Sushila and her brother. Sushila started working to support the family. She had to help her mother meet the educational expenses of her brother, who was studying in an engineering college. That was why she had taken up the job at St. Xavier's College. And now, she had given up her job on a matter of principle, even though they were all struggling to meet her brother's expenses. Her mother was worried when she came to know that Sushila had given up her job, but when the reason for her action was explained, she did not hesitate to support her daughter.

However, they had to find some income without delay.

Sushila was offered a job at Glaxo. But at the interview she had to admit that she had not learned typing, and so, she was not accepted. She attended an interview for a job at Blue Star where she told the interviewer that she was really interested in going for higher studies. The chief executive officer was impressed by her honesty and sincerity and congratulated her and wished her all the best in life, even though the job was not offered to her. Still, she wanted to know why Sushila was looking for a job if her intention was to pursue her studies. When she came to know about the responsibilities she had to bear, including her brother's education, the officer wanted to help her by giving her some work.

Sushila was too young to be given the job which her qualifications demanded. So she was allowed to play badminton and represent the company at different tournaments. She was paid for it and the chief executive officer of the company promised Sushila that she would be absorbed into the company once she attained the required age.

Concern for His Wife

The Asian Games, also known as ASIAD, were held in 1982 when Balagurusamy and Sushila were in Delhi. People were watching the games on television sets at their houses in Delhi. Colour television had just made its appearance in India. Balagurusamy was not in a position to buy a television for himself, and he was not interested in purchasing one either for it had no place in their simple life.

It was October 1984, and televisions all over the world were showing Indira Gandhi falling to the assassin's bullets. Sushila had to go to the neighbour's house to watch it.

Balagurusamy suddenly felt sorry that he was not able to get a television for his wife.

It was at this time that he received his first official royalty, a sum of thirteen thousand rupees, for one of the books that he had written. He did not waste any time thinking about what to do with it. He bought a television set and presented it to his wife.

Thus, after having worked at different companies, Sushila joined the TTTI at Bhopal as an assistant professor. 'My mother used to say that we should do our best to excel in our work. But she advised us not to let our success go to our head. My mother was not highly educated. That made her decide that her children should study as much as possible. She insisted on us being truthful in our thoughts and sincere in whatever we did. My mother is my guide in all matters,' said Sushila in one of the interviews for 'Anna FM', a community radio launched by Dr Balagurusamy.

Sushila had wanted to be a journalist. But her mother insisted that she would not be able to meet all the different situations that she would have to face as she travelled widely as a journalist.

Then she had also desired to appear for the IAS examination and enter the civil service. Again, her mother had an objection. She believed that if girls rose to occupy high positions, like that of a district collector, it would be challenging to find suitable marriage alliances.

Crime and Punishment

There was a worker at the TTTI, Bhopal, by the name of Haneefa. Haneefa was asked to clean the floor of the room used by Prof. Sushila. But he refused to do it. She then took the cloth from Haneefa and swept the floor herself. The authorities had already received many complaints against Haneefa. They had decided to get Sushila's opinion too and dismiss Haneefa. When they asked Prof. Sushila whether she had any complaints against Haneefa, she said, 'Haneefa is doing his work well.'

Haneefa did not lose his job. When the man learnt that she had given a reasonable opinion about him despite his refusal to clean her room, he changed his attitude and did his work more diligently. Prof. Sushila believed that it was better to give a person a chance to correct himself than accuse him and punish him. This helped Haneefa learn a valuable lesson and keep his job too.

'I was lucky to get Balagurusamy as my husband,' said Sushila. 'He is a genius. He will excel in whatever he does. I will never interfere in his work. But once he has completed a task, I remind him that it is not the end. There are more things that we have to do. I believe he is happy with the encouragement I give him,' Sushila stated. She has also clarified that her husband had always encouraged her and supported her in all her activities. She further said, 'There is a popular saying that behind every successful man, there is a woman. But in my case, it should be the other way round. Behind every successful woman, there is a man.'

When Balagurusamy was the vice-chancellor of Anna University, Sushila offered her voluntary services to the university. When the university started a community FM radio, it was challenging to get enough material to broadcast in the initial stages. Sushila came forward with suggestions and help. Her work helped in making the radio programme thrive. Prof. Sreedhar, the media department director at the campus, expressed his indebtedness to her. 'She encouraged the students to meet people from the lower strata of society and find out the problems that they faced. These should be made the topic for discussion in the community radio programmes. Then young people would know about the difficulties that these people had to face in their day-to-day life. Let the students realize that, with the money that they spend for a pair of shoes, a low-income family would be able to meet all the needs of the members. When they have to plan for their future, these revelations will stand them in good stead.'

Sreedhar took such practical advice that he got from Sushila very seriously. He entrusted one hundred of his students to meet poor people, find out the problems that they had to face and suggest remedies. This proved to be a successful campaign. The people started listening to the community radio with interest and enthusiasm. Sushila took part in ten interviews, each lasting one hour, on different topics broadcast on the community radio of Anna University.

Like Balagurusamy, Sushila also had to face many difficulties in her life. But with hard work and self-confidence, she was able to overcome all obstacles and take postgraduate degrees in English literature and management studies. After that, she did her doctorate in human resource development.

18

Good Tidings in the Path of Life

Be born with fame if birth you want,
if not of birth you must not vaunt.

—Thirukkural 236

The TTTI at Bhopal provided training to teachers in civil, mechanical and electrical engineering, management, psychology and research. Balagurusamy was in the electrical engineering department, while Sushila was in educational research.

All the members of the faculty were divided into task groups. There were task groups such as the evaluation task group, management task group, teaching and learning process task group,' etc. Each faculty had to join two of these groups as members. Balagurusamy had taken the teaching and learning process task group and management task group.

In the year 1978, TTTI Bhopal established a computer centre with an HP 9000 computer system to provide training to the teachers under the United Nations Development Programme (UNDP). As per the scheme, training had to be given to the teachers for developing computer programs in BASIC language. BASIC is an acronym that stands for Beginners' All-purpose Symbolic Instruction Code. It is a general-purpose, high-level programming language whose design philosophy emphasizes ease of use.

As Balagurusamy had experience of working with computers for developing software at BHEL, he was entrusted with the task of teaching programming. With this, Balagurusamy became the manifestation of a 'complete computer man'. This new responsibility changed the course of his learning and knowledge and that of his life.

Teachers in engineering colleges and polytechnics in Madhya Pradesh, Gujarat and Maharashtra had to be given training in computer programming. But in 1970s, no textbooks were available for computer training. Balagurusamy had to depend on the manuals given along with the HP 9000 computer. When he was teaching BASIC programming using the manuals, the students complained that they were finding it difficult to understand what was being taught and suggested that it would be helpful if detailed notes were given on the subject. So Balagurusamy started preparing detailed notes on BASIC programming. These notes later became the contents of the first book that Balagurusamy wrote on computers.

India was a member of the international forum known as the Colombo Plan. One of the main aims of the forum was technical cooperation for development among member countries. The four TTTIs of India were included in this programme. As per the scheme, every year, two people from each of the TTTIs had to go to Britain for a six-month training programme in teaching and learning. In 1979, Balagurusamy was chosen to go from Bhopal TTTI. So he left for London in December 1979.

It was the first journey overseas for Balagurusamy. From Bhopal, he travelled to Bombay by train; then he took the eleven-hour Air India flight to London. He landed at Heathrow Airport in London on 30 December 1979. The cold was biting. As he had bought some winter clothes from Bombay, he could withstand the freezing temperatures. The British Council which hosted the programme, had arranged for his transit stay in a hotel in London. The training was to start on 1 January 1980, at the Roehampton Institute of Higher Education. But Balagurusamy found it too cold to even get out of his room. It was the worst winter in the UK in fifty years. No vehicles were on the streets.

Balagurusamy joined training only on 10 January, when the snow and rain had cleared slightly. At Roehampton Institute, hostel facilities were shared by men and women. Balagurusamy was facing such a situation for the first time in his life.

Only Balagurusamy and another teacher, Dr Banthia, had doctorate degrees in engineering among those who had come for the training. By the time he had attended the training classes for a month, he had found that all the portions were what he had already studied. He could also imagine that it would be the same in the coming months. So he felt that this training would be of no use and decided to return home. He informed the training coordinator about his decision. Dr Banthia also agreed with his decision and was ready to leave.

The training coordinator felt they might give their programme a negative report and so said, 'Don't go back now. You can attend five or six international conferences held in some of the important universities in the UK and submit a detailed report. That can be considered as a part of the training. I will make all the arrangements for it.'

Balagurusamy was happy to accept the coordinator's suggestion. So Balagurusamy and Banthia participated in the international conferences held in prestigious universities in England, Scotland and Wales. This gave them the rare opportunity to meet and become acquainted with experts in the field of education as well as those who were engaged in research. They both were back in London by May after attending all the conferences. Balagurusamy spent the rest of the training period developing software for computer-aided learning (CAL) using BASIC language. He left for Bhopal in June 1980 after completing the training.

While he was working as a trainer in the TTTI, the teachers used to conduct seminars at various institutions in the western region. For one of these seminars, Balagurusamy went to Ahmedabad to conduct a workshop for polytechnic teachers. As he could not get a first-class ticket, he travelled by air-conditioned (AC) coach. The fare of the AC coach was slightly more than that of the non-AC first class ticket. After the journey, Balagurusamy submitted the papers for reimbursement of fares and other allowances connected with the travel.

The next day, the accountant called Balagurusamy and pointed out, 'You have shown more than what you are allowed to spend. You are allowed to travel only by non-AC first class. But you have travelled in the AC coach, spending more money.' He also said that only the director had the authority to approve the sanction for the higher amount.

Prof. Mani, who had played the father's role at Balagurusamy's wedding, was the director at that time. The papers were sent to him for approval. He examined the statement of expenses submitted by Balagurusamy. The accountant had noted that the amount was more than what could be sanctioned. Prof. Mani sent the papers back with a message that it was impossible to pay anything more than what was allowed. He instructed the accountant to pay what was permissible. The director did not sanction the payment that Balagurusamy had claimed, though he had the authority to do so.

Balagurusamy went to the director and said, 'I travelled on the authorization given by the institute. I had to take the AC ticket as the first class ticket was unavailable. As I had to reach the place on time to conduct the seminar, I took the AC ticket, paying extra money. I have submitted all the papers to show that.'

'Only the amount allowed by the government can be reimbursed,' Mani said sternly.

Balagurusamy took the bills back from his table and tore them into pieces in front of the director. His eyes were burning in anger. 'I don't want any money. Consider it as a free journey.' He then left the room, submitting an application for leave of absence for a month.

When they were at home in the evening, Sushila tried to find out what had happened. 'Yes, if we are honest, we have to listen to all that others say. And to add to it, he had to quote the rules. So I took leave for a month.' Balagurusamy was still angry.

'But what will you do at home for one month? You cannot sit idle even for a minute. It will only be a waste of time,' said Sushila in a calm voice, but her disapproval was evident.

'No, Sushila. Do you think I am going to waste this one month?' Balagurusamy responded.

Sushila waited for some time before getting up to leave the room. 'I cannot imagine what you would do at home for one month,' she said.

'Look here,' Balagurusamy said as he got up, 'I will write a book in this one month.'

'Will you be able to do it in that time?' Sushila asked sceptically.

'Wait and see. I will complete the book in one month,' Balagurusamy said confidently.

Sushila concealed her delight. She had received assurances that he would do something without wasting his time and that the leave he had taken would result in the birth of something useful for others.

First Book on BASIC in India

One fine morning, a marketing executive from Macmillan Publishers visited TTTI Bhopal and the librarian directed him to meet Prof. Balagurusamy. While talking to Balagurusamy, he noticed the draft copy on BASIC programming on the table. After glancing through the manuscript, he expressed interest in publishing it as a book and took it with him. But there was no response from Macmillan for almost six months. So Balagurusamy sent another copy of the manuscript to McGraw Hill. As they had already seen his work on reliability engineering, they readily agreed to publish it.

Thus, the first book on BASIC programming was published in India by McGraw Hill Publishing Co. Ltd.

Sushila attended college regularly while Balagurusamy remained at home and worked on the book—without wasting even a second. Before the month ended, the text on BASIC programming language was ready. Considering the inspiration and support that Sushila had rendered in completing the book, Balagurusamy dedicated it to her. He rejoined the college after a month, but somehow he realized that he had lost all interest in continuing to work there. He was convinced that his enthusiasm and curiosity were not to be limited within the four walls of that institute.

A big advertisement for the National Institute of Information Technology (NIIT) appeared in some leading newspapers around that time. Balagurusamy was interested in working in information technology, and therefore he met R.S. Pawar, the managing director of NIIT in New Delhi, and expressed his desire to work for them. Pawar was happy and said, 'Dr Balagurusamy, we are obliged to use the knowledge and experience of an expert like you.'

Balagurusamy had one condition: his wife must also be employed there. That was also accepted immediately.

Thus, in the first week of September 1982, Balagurusamy and Sushila joined NIIT. At that time, NIIT was functioning in a small building in Safdarjung Enclave in New Delhi. Balagurusamy was appointed as the manager of training and education, while Sushila was appointed as its business executive. Balagurusamy was entrusted with the task of designing curricula for new courses on computers as well as preparing teaching materials for them.

At that time, NIIT had entered into an agreement with the Advanced System Institute (ASI) in America. ASI provided notes and videotapes for training on computer programming and applications. Initially, NIIT was offering training courses based on these materials. When the video classes were going on, the teacher would also be present in the class. He would switch off the video and then explain the lessons. Questions and doubts raised by the students were also answered in this manner. Prof. Balagurusamy was the first person to hold such video classes for young students in December 1982 at NIIT, Delhi.

Similar training programmes were also conducted for corporate executives. Balagurusamy led a seminar on 'Using Computers as Management Tool (UCMT)' for the officers of BHEL units in New Delhi and a training programme on COBOL (Common Business Oriented Language) for the officers of the Life Insurance Corporation (LIC) in the northern region in Chandigarh. Another major training programme, 'Using COBOL for Business Applications', for executives of Hindustan Computers Limited (HCL) was initiated and coordinated by Prof. Balagurusamy.

By the middle of 1983, NIIT had opened training centres in important cities all over the country. Many college students and working executives joined the various courses offered at these centres. Thus, Balagurusamy, as a part of NIIT, played a major role in promoting computer literacy in India early in the 1980s, back when personal computers (PCs) had not yet been introduced in India.

India's First Symposium on Use of Computers in Education

While working at NIIT, Balagurusamy organized a national symposium on 'Computers in Education and Training (COMET),'

> in collaboration with IIT Delhi in March 1983. The main topic, which was exhaustively discussed, was how computers and information technology could be utilized in education and training. Prof. Ramaswamy Iyer, director of IIM Calcutta; Prof. S. Sampath, director of IIT Kanpur; and Dr N. Seshagiri, director general of National Informatics Centre were also among the 300 experts who spoke at the symposium. It was the first meeting on using computers in education to be held in India.

It was during his time at NIIT that Balagurusamy prepared the manuscript for the book on FORTRAN IV programming and submitted it to McGraw Hill for publication. He also developed a working manual on COBOL programming for HCL employees, which was later published as a book by Macmillan Publishers in New Delhi.

Although Prof. Balagurusamy was actively engaged in developing courses and conducting training programmes for young boys and girls, he was alarmed and dissatisfied by the commercialization of education at NIIT. He was constantly contemplating on how he could make his knowledge useful through public service.

19
Andhra Pradesh Beckons

*All lands and towns are learner's own,
why not till death (do) learnings go on!*

—Thirukkural 397

Balagurusamy had decided to move away from NIIT. One day he went out for dinner with some friends to Andhra Bhavan in New Delhi. In those days, the Andhra Bhavan canteen was very popular for non-vegetarian food. As they were waiting for the food and discussing something related to computers at their table, a gentleman from the nearby table approached Balagurusamy.

'Are you from Tamil Nadu, Sir?'

Balagurusamy turned to him, 'Yes, Is there anything…?'

'From your conversation, I gather that you are an expert on computers,' the gentleman said.

'Yes. I am not a great expert in computers. But I have been working in that area for the last few years,' Balagurusamy replied.

The gentleman was a senior officer of the Andhra Pradesh government. This was when N.T. Rama Rao was the chief minister of Andhra Pradesh. Chief Minister Rama Rao was keen on ushering development into his state. He also wanted to initiate several welfare schemes for the benefit of the poor and rural populations.

The officer continued. 'Can you come to Andhra Pradesh and advise us on how computer technology can be utilized to improve the government's administration?'

Balagurusamy thought about it. 'Let me have some more details. Then we can think about it.'

'Thank you, Sir. We will get back to you soon after discussing with our CM.'

One week later, Balagurusamy got a call from the Special Officer of Andhra Bhavan to meet Dr Y. Venugopal Reddy, planning secretary, Andhra Pradesh government, and T.L. Shankar, the finance secretary, at Andhra Bhavan. When he met them in the evening, he found both the officers to be very gracious, outspoken gentlemen. They said, 'We heard about you and your interest in computers. Our chief minister desires to popularize the use of computers in our state and wants you to give the officers some training. It would be great if you could visit him and give the details of the steps involved in doing that.'

As Balagurusamy and Sushila were waiting for an opportunity to serve the public at large, he readily accepted the invitation. Thus, Balagurusamy and Sushila met Chief Minister N.T. Rama Rao and held discussions with him at the Andra Pradesh Secretariat.

'Can you come here and take up the post of IT Advisor?' the chief minister asked him. Shankar, the finance secretary, was also present there at that time.

Balagurusamy was hesitant about accepting a government job directly. If he became a government servant, he might not have permission to publish books. He had made plans to write many books. He spoke to T.L. Shankar about it and Shankar had a solution. Shankar also held the post of the director of the Institute of Public Enterprise (IPE), a central government organization in Hyderabad.

'You may join (the) IPE as a professor of computer science. You can also work as the IT Advisor for the state government,' Shankar suggested.

Balagurusamy and Sushila readily agreed to the suggestion.

Thus, in December 1983, Balagurusamy joined the IPE as a professor of computer science. T.L. Shankar established the new computers and information technology department at the IPE. Balagurusamy was made the chairman of that department. He thus became one of the first few computer science professors in the country.

Andhra Pradesh Must be Number One

One day, Chief Minister Rama Rao called T.L. Shankar, Dr Y.V. Reddy and Balagurusamy to discuss the use of computers in district administration and to monitor the implementation of welfare projects at the district level. At that time, he expressed his desire that Andhra Pradesh must lead the other states in the country in its use of computers for government administration.

Dr Reddy immediately constituted a committee under Prof. Balagurusamy to identify the states where computers were installed and to study the nature and extent of the use of those computers for government administration. Accordingly, the committee visited the states of Tamil Nadu, Karnataka, Kerala, Maharashtra and Madhya Pradesh. Most of them had installed some kind of data processing machines to be used by their Bureaus of Economics and Statistics (BES) to maintain various types of data. Nothing was happening in terms of the application of computers in administration. Further, during the discussions with various state BES officials, the visiting team found that none had any plans for implementing computer-based projects.

Although the committee did not get anything useful, members were happy to note that Andhra Pradesh would be leading other states in the country if the ideas of the chief minister were implemented, thus making his dream come true.

On the advice of Prof. Balagurusamy, the state government issued orders making computer literacy compulsory for all its employees. N.T. Rama Rao inaugurated the first phase of that training programme. Balagurusamy became a close friend of Rama Rao soon, and he was also appointed as the Science and Technology Advisor.

Shankar suggested that, apart from government employees, all those who were working in government undertakings also must be trained in the use of computers. So Balagurusamy started computer training programmes for the executives and staff of all the establishments under the government, including organizations like Hyderabad Allwyn, the

AP Cooperative Bank, the AP Financial Corporation and AP Industrial Development Corporation.

NTR'S TWENTY-FIVE POINT PROGRAMME

The Twenty-Point Programme of the then Prime Minister, Indira Gandhi, was being implemented at that time. Adding to that the five points emphasized by N.T. Rama Rao, Andhra Pradesh decided to implement the Twenty-Five Point Programme. The district collectors were entrusted with implementing the programme in their districts. Whatever was being done by the district collectors also had to be recorded. Each month, the collectors had to submit a report regarding the progress of the implementation—with details of the completed programmes and those that were incomplete, along with estimates of the time required to implement the pending ones. The chief minister wanted this district-wise information with rankings on the first week of every month. The planning department found the task very difficult to implement on time.

Balagurusamy suggested the use computers for all this work. There were no CDs or pen drives in those days. All the details were recorded on 8-inch floppy disks. These had to reach the office of the planning department by the 5th of the following month. After thorough scrutiny, details of the best districts, those that remained backward, and new suggestions for implementation would be made and the districts would be evaluated. The three best districts would be marked. These detailed reports had to reach the chief minister by the 7th of every month.

First Computer Exhibition

Computers had just made their entry into India. Chief Minister N.T. Rama Rao had introduced computers in Andhra Pradesh mainly on the advice of Balagurusamy. People had no awareness or knowledge about computers and their use in those days.

'The next era will be that of computers. Government officers and workers, and the common people have to get some idea of

the way to use computers and become aware of the advantages arising out of their use. It will be useful if we hold an exhibition for this purpose,' Balagurusamy said, laying his suggestion before the chief minister.

The suggestion was accepted.

A computer exhibition was held for the first time at the Public Gardens in Hyderabad in March 1985. The three-day exhibition was inaugurated by Prof. M.G.K. Menon, member of the Central Planning Commission, at a function presided over by Chief Minister N.T. Rama Rao.

This exhibition attracted large crowds on all three days and proved to be very useful for officials and the public at large.

Thus, Andhra Pradesh became the first state where the work done in all the districts was recorded on the computer. Balagurusamy visited all the districts in Andhra Pradesh in connection with this work. Training on computers was given to all the officers in various districts. For this, computer training centres were started in all the districts.

Under a detailed plan proposal by Prof. Balagurusamy, the installation of PCs was initiated in all government offices from April 1984 onwards. As a part of the plan, the first computer was installed in the residence of Chief Minister N.T. Rama Rao in the first week of April 1984. It was the first time in India that a computer was being installed in the residence of a political leader. Over the next three months, PCs were installed in all the secretariat departments and district headquarters. Within a few months, laypeople too became aware of the use of computers.

Balagurusamy always believed that training should be 'top down' and that implementation should be 'bottom up.' Thus, he organized a symposium on the 'Use of IT in Government Administration' which was held on 16 August 1984, in Hyderabad. It was organised as part of the efforts to impart training to the state government's top officials, including IAS and IPS officers. T.L. Shankar, Y. Venugopal Reddy and many high-ranking officers participated in the programme. The meeting was inaugurated by Shravan Kumar, IAS, chief secretary of

Andhra Pradesh. The main purpose of the symposium was to show how computerization could be effective in the administration of different departments.

But the symposium did not proceed as planned.

20

Viral Attack on Democracy

Though fate is against fulfilment,
hard labour has ready payment.

—Thirukkural 619

The discussions at the symposium had been going on for almost an hour when the Chief Secretary Shravan Kumar got a message that N.T. Rama Rao had been removed from the chief minister's post. Bhaskara Rao, a senior member of the Telugu Desam Party, met the governor, Thakur Ram Lal, claiming that he could prove his majority in the assembly. He was proclaimed the new chief minister, even though Rama Rao had a majority in the assembly. It was rumoured then that a political coup was enacted to remove Rao. Rao led a protest march to the residence of the governor with the members of the assembly who supported him.

The symposium that Balagurusamy had organized was disrupted soon after the inauguration. Political uncertainty prevailed in Andhra Pradesh for more than a month. The programme for information technology that Rama Rao had wanted to implement in the state also had to be stalled.

Rama Rao, once again, became the chief minister after overcoming many crises. Rama Rao then dissolved the assembly and called for fresh elections. In the elections that were held, along with elections for Parliament, Rao came back with greater power. And Balagurusamy once again became the advisor to the government on science and technology.

Balagurusamy had ensured that some general knowledge about computers was provided even to those in the lower rungs of government service. This proved to be beneficial as it allayed their fear that they would lose their jobs after computerization. They realized that it was possible to complete their work on time with the help of the machines. So there was no resistance against computerization from government employees.

Balagurusamy was happy and interested in working as the advisor on science and technology in the Rama Rao administration. There were some specific reasons for it. Rama Rao had dreams and hopes of doing things for the welfare of society. He selected those who were efficient and committed to implementing his goals. Dr Balagurusamy was one of them.

Andhra Pradesh soon became the first state in India to computerize its government offices. This was implemented by Balagurusamy. The chief minister gave him unstinted support in this venture. As per the advice provided by Balagurusamy, all the universities in Andhra Pradesh started offering computer science courses like Bachelors in Computer Application and Masters in Computer Application, with special funds provided for by the government.

Rama Rao also wanted to introduce video-based teaching in government schools in the state. A committee was formed to chalk out a plan to offer video-based classes and recommend suitable projection systems. Sushil Kumar, Secretary, Industries Department; U.V. Warlu, Chairman, Andhra Pradesh Electronic Development Corporation; Dr P.L. Sanjeeva Reddy, Chairman, Andhra Pradesh Industrial Development Corporation, and Prof. Balagurusamy were the committee members.

Tenders were invited for the supply of projectors to the schools and five companies participated. The chief minister instructed the participating companies to hold a demonstration of their products at his residence. After seeing the demonstration, he decided that the projector belonging to the fifth company was the best. It must have been easy for the chief minister to identify a good projector considering his decades of experience in the world of cinema. But there was a problem—the system he had selected was the costliest among the five. Governments usually had to choose the cheapest option to minimize expenses. If costly projectors were bought, the Opposition in the Legislative Assembly would challenge it in court. When the officers pointed out this difficulty, the chief minister responded: 'I wish to give the best equipment for the students in our state. I stand by my decision. I believe in doing the right thing. Laws are all made by us. We have the responsibility to change them when required.'

The officers were in a dilemma. They had to adopt a new strategy to overcome this difficulty. They cancelled the tender and invited new tenders. Some changes were made to the conditions as well. In short, they managed to change the conditions so that they could buy the projectors that had been approved by the chief minister.

The computer revolution was spreading all over India, and it was no wonder that Andhra Pradesh became the leading state in computerization when the chief minister was so determined; he readily listened to the expert advice given by Dr Y.V. Reddy and Prof. Balagurusamy. As the conditions were amicable, Balagurusamy continued working in Andhra Pradesh for a long time.

During this period, he was also able to bring out many books on computers.

'There was a deep-rooted belief that computerization would take away employment opportunities. We should be thankful to Dr Balagurusamy for proving, through practical demonstrations, that this was a baseless fear,' said one of the former officers in the state secretariat.

Many other states also started following what Balagurusamy was doing in Andhra Pradesh.

The services rendered by Balagurusamy in the application of computers can be seen when we look at the history of the development of e-governance in Andhra Pradesh and the development of computer science in the country.

MGR's Interest

Computers and split ACs were installed in the Andhra Pradesh Secretariat for the first time in India during the chief ministership of N.T. Rama Rao. On one occasion, Tamil Nadu's chief minister, M.G. Ramachandran, a close friend of Rama Rao, was a guest at his house. It was then that the Tamil Nadu Chief Minister saw the computers and split ACs in Rama Rao's residence. He had never seen an AC unit working so silently before that. With surprise apparent on his face, he enquired who had done all this work, and NTR replied: 'A computer scientist from your state, Dr Balagurusamy.'

MGR, M.G. Ramachandran, wanted to meet Balagurusamy. But Balagurusamy could not meet the Tamil Nadu Chief Minister immediately due to some other commitments.

Later, when he went to Tamil Nadu to meet him, MGR had already left for America to undergo medical treatment. So he was requested to meet Mr C. Ponnaian, the education minister, and Mr Srinivasan, the director of technical education. He talked to them about the computerization programmes implemented by the Andhra Pradesh government. Balagurusamy hoped that these details would be passed on to the chief minister and he would receive a positive response so that he could do similar service in his state. But what came next was the news of the death of the chief minister.

Thus the dream that Balagurusamy had cherished also came to nothing.

FIRST RADIO TALK ON COMPUTER USE

For the first time in India, a talk on computer usage was broadcast from the Hyderabad Radio station. Prof. Balagurusamy was the first person to deliver a talk in English which was followed by Y. Venugopal Reddy's in Telugu.

Rajiv Gandhi became the Prime Minister of India in 1984. P. Chidambaram was a Minister of State in the Prime Minister's Office and was in charge of the Department of Personnel. He implemented a countrywide programme to give expert training to IAS officers who had completed more than five years of service.

IAS officers were assured of a promotion every five years, but many of them could not acquire the ability to match such elevations. The training programme that Chidambaram envisaged was meant to give the officers an idea about the innovations in the world of management. He suggested two types of training: Horizontal Training and Vertical Training. Horizontal Training was meant for IAS officers of the same rank, working in various departments; this was designed as a separate training for the secretaries, joint secretaries and district collectors. Vertical Training was meant to be given to all officers, from top to bottom, in each department.

These were new ideas, and four centres for imparting such training were identified, including the IPE in Hyderabad. P. Chidambaram inaugurated the training programme at the IPE. Dr Balagurusamy was among those who were selected to impart training.

Many senior IAS officers, including central and state government secretaries, participated in the training programmes. Among them were Lakshmi Pranesh and T.V. Antony from Tamil Nadu. Those who had completed the training were required to report to the central government. All those who submitted the report chose Balagurusamy as one of the best trainers.

One of the trainee officers from Punjab, Navaneet Kaur, was the secretary of the department of science and technology. She spoke to the chief minister of Punjab, Surjit Singh Barnala, about the efficiency and other praiseworthy qualities of Balagurusamy. Based on this, Barnala requested Balagurusamy to be the science and technology advisor to the Government of Punjab. Balagurusamy accepted the offer and acted as the advisor to the Punjab government for a year, while continuing to serve in Andhra Pradesh.

Balagurusamy took the lead in installing computers in the office of the Governor of Punjab, Sidhartha Shankar Ray. The Punjab government wanted him to work in Punjab full-time as the secretary of science and technology, but as the Khalistan agitation was lashing that state at that time, Balagurusamy had to decline the offer.

Balagurusamy also served the Government of Rajasthan in the capacity of an advisor in science and technology for a brief period. During this time, computers were installed in the office of Chief Minister Haridev Joshy.

Lakshmi Pranesh, who had attended one of the training programmes, later became chief secretary of Tamil Nadu. She talked to Selvi J. Jayalalithaa about Balagurusamy, and his expertise and this later led to the friendly relationship that he was able to establish with Jayalalithaa.

Another critical achievement of Balagurusamy while serving in Andhra Pradesh was organizing many international conferences through which India's development in science and technology came to the notice of the world. One of the most important of such conferences was the International Conference on Application of Artificial Intelligence, held in 1989. More than 500 delegates from over 30 countries participated in it. Prime Minister Rajiv Gandhi was expected to inaugurate the conference, but he could not do it due to unforeseen circumstances. R. Rajamani, the secretary of the department of electronics, Government of India, inaugurated the meeting in his stead.

Balagurusamy wanted to invite Edward Albert Feigenbaum, the world-famous scientist also known as the father of artificial intelligence (AI), to the conference. All his friends discouraged Balagurusamy, saying it was impossible to get him to attend. Balagurusamy persisted and surprised them by getting him to give the keynote address at the conference by just sending him a letter.

Balagurusamy got all the papers that were presented at the conference published in a special edition book, adhering to international standards. Macmillan Publishers published this. Experts in the office of the United Nations in Vienna scrutinized the gist of the research papers in this edition and they were full of praise for Balagurusamy, the chief editor of the publication. Balagurusamy continued to organize conferences on computer science every year under the banner of the Indian Computing Congress. Thousands of students, research scholars and teachers benefited through their participation in these conferences.

Loyal to His Motherland

Macmillan published the papers presented at the international conference on AI organized in Hyderabad by Balagurusamy, in *the form of a book. The experts of the United Nations Industrial Development Corporation (UNIDO) in Vienna had cited the book as one that maintained very high standards and made an essential contribution to AI. In recognition of Balagurusamy's contribution to AI, UNIDO wanted to use his services in Vienna where he was invited to work as an advisor on AI for a salary of $15,000 a month.*

But Balagurusamy was not ready to leave his country to go to Vienna. He gave up the offer for the sake of his motherland. He was ready to serve as an advisor on expert system to UNIDO from India. An expert system is a software which behaves like an expert. Expert systems are designed and developed to provide expert advice in areas such as medicine, agriculture, tax calculations and many more. Accordingly, he served as Advisor on Expert Systems to UNIDO while staying in Hyderabad. He was paid $2,000 a month for his efforts.

As problems rose in the Telugu Desam Party, leadership was taken over by Chandrababu Naidu, nephew of Rama Rao. By the end of 1995, Rama Rao was out of power. As he was a close friend of Rama Rao, Balagurusamy did not want to continue his services in Andhra Pradesh. So he left his position as the advisor to the Government of Andhra Pradesh.

While he was advisor to the Government of Andhra Pradesh, many achievements had been recorded. Notable among them is the establishment of Andhra Pradesh Technology Services Limited (APTS), the southern regional centre (SRC) of the National Informatics Centre (NIC) at Hyderabad and the information technology department of Andhra Pradesh. For the first time in India, department for information technology was opened under a state government. APTS was the principal establishment of a state government that had brought in e-governance. Similarly, when the central government thought of establishing a regional centre of the NIC, it was under Balagurusamy's initiative that it was brought to Hyderabad.

Among the books that Prof. Balagurusamy wrote while he was

advisor in Andhra Pradesh, experts consider *Programming in ANSI C* as the best. Balagurusamy named his book *Programming in ANSI C* as experts in computer science expect any publication on computer languages, like C, to keep to the standards set by the American National Standard Institute (ANSI). Balagurusamy's book gained prominence worldwide even though others written by world-famous experts in computer science were available. There is an interesting story behind the writing of this book.

THE STORY OF THE C-PROGRAMMING BOOK

Balagurusamy had to travel to Delhi on matters connected with the government. On one occasion, as he reached the airport to come back to Hyderabad, it was announced that there would be a delay of nine hours. Balagurusamy went to the bookshop and looked for something to help him get through those nine hours of waiting. He saw a book on C-programming, written by Brain Kernighan and Dennis Ritchie, and bought it. He found it very difficult to understand. He wondered how students would benefit from it if even a teacher found it difficult to understand. He had the feeling that C programming should be explained in a language that would make sense even to students from rural India. This was what made him write the book on programming in ANSI C.

21
PSG Invites EBG

*By noble forbearance, vanquish
the proud that have caused you anguish.*

—Thirukkural 158

The phone rang, and as he answered it, a voice asked, 'Is that Professor Balagurusamy?'

It was a call from PSG College of Technology, Coimbatore.

'Sir, the PSG Trust wishes to honour you with the "Distinguished PSG Alumni" award. We would like you to come in person and receive the award.' This was the essence of the phone call. He was not thrilled to hear from PSG, but he said, 'I have to think about it. I will call you later.'

With great bitterness and sorrow, Balagurusamy had once left the hallowed halls of PSG College. Now he was unsure about how he should react to this invitation. So, he discussed the matter with his wife.

'Isn't it great that the same institution that had once insulted you is now calling you back there to honour you? It is better to accept that award.' Sushila's opinion was clear and definite.

After long deliberation, Balagurusamy decided to accept the invitation. Had it not been for his wife's love and persuasion, perhaps he would not have accepted that award. As he intimated his willingness to accept the award, Prof. S. Subramanian, principal of PSG College of Technology, came to Hyderabad to invite him in person. Prof. Subramanian had been Balagurusamy's teacher and hostel warden when he was a student there. Later, the college authorities informed him that arrangements for his stay had been made at the guest house of the college and that they were sending him tickets to fly to Coimbatore.

But Balagurusamy was not ready to accept any hospitality offered by the college. So he informed them that he had made arrangements for his stay and travel himself.

They arranged for a grand function for the award ceremony on the evening of 25 January 1994, the Founders' Day of the PSG Trust. Dr M. Anandakrishnan, vice-chancellor of Anna University, was the chief guest and presented Balagurusamy the award. Trustees of PSG, many of Balagurusamy's teachers and a galaxy of guests from Coimbatore, were present at the function.

After dinner, Karthikeyan, Managing Trustee of the PSG Group of Institutions, made arrangements to take Balagurusamy to the hotel. Balagurusamy politely declined the offer and went back to the hotel in a taxi he had hired. But Karthikeyan accompanied him to the hotel. On the way to the hotel, Karthikeyan informed him that they planned to start an Institute of Management Studies under the PSG Group and make it a national-level institute. They were looking for an excellent director to head the new institution.

'That is a good decision,' Balagurusamy said. 'We need good institutions for imparting management education in Tamil Nadu. I will inform you as soon as I find someone suitable to be the director,' he added.

'No, Sir, we want you to take responsibility,' Karthikeyan said.

Balagurusamy could not help but laugh out loud. 'Sir, I am an expert in computer science and not in management. How can I take charge of a management institute?'

'It is not just that. The person who takes charge as the director must have wide experience, leadership qualities, managerial insight and honesty. That is why we are inviting you,' Karthikeyan said to him.

'Let that be; I will inform you when I find somebody more qualified and suited for the post.' Balagurusamy did not give in. Karthikeyan, however, insisted that he consider the request.

Balagurusamy discussed the matter with Sushila as soon as he reached Hyderabad.

'See, things are improving. Those who insulted and caused you pain once have now honoured you with an award and are offering you a high-ranking job. There is no need to think any more about it. You should accept it.' Sushila expressed her opinion patiently.

Balagurusamy thus decided to return to Coimbatore. Karthikeyan was pleased to hear of his decision and arranged for a meeting at Coimbatore to discuss more details. This time, Balagurusamy accepted the tickets that Karthikeyan had sent and the offer for accommodation at their guest house.

Prof. S. Subramanian, the principal of PSG Tech earlier and now the vice-chancellor of Bharathiar University and C.R. Swaminathan, chief executive officer of the PSG Group of Institutions, visited him at the guest house in the evening, as instructed by Karthikeyan.

They informed Balagurusamy of Karthikeyan's dreams and plans for the management institute. He wanted the institute to be one of the best in the country. Balagurusamy disclosed what he was planning to do and informed them what they would have to do for the institute. At last, they came to the question of what Balagurusamy wanted for himself.

'We have a lot of books. My wife is engaged in research and teaching. And we have some pets. So we will need an independent house with a proper compound wall,' Balagurusamy said.

The two men representing the PSG Group of Institutions looked uneasy upon hearing this. 'No separate houses have been given even to the principals of PSG Tech and PSG Medical College. The PSG Trust does not have such a scheme. We are not sure whether the management will be ready to change their policy for you,' they explained.

Balagurusamy, too, made his stand clear: he would not be interested in staying in a rented house. So the representatives offered to discuss the matter with the authorities and give him a definite answer.

Then Balagurusamy came up with the request for a car and a driver. Though the two men were hesitant about that too, they promised to raise this also with the authorities. They said that PSG had no provision to provide a car and driver to the heads of institutions. Swaminathan said to Balagurusamy, 'Sir, we understand you already have two cars.'

'Yes, I do. But it will enhance the image and prestige of the PSG Institute if its director travels by the institute car,' Balagurusamy quipped.

'How much do you expect as your salary?' was their next question. They now expected him to demand some lakhs.

'I won't make any demands about my salary. You can give me whatever you feel is adequate. But just remember, that when I am asked about my salary by someone else, the answer that I give should not bring disgrace to the institution.'

The two men were not only surprised but also perplexed. Hearing the first two demands of the man, they considered Balagurusamy as someone greedy for money. But his words about the salary made them change their opinion.

Karthikeyan was informed about Balagurusamy's demands. Karthikeyan sent a car to bring Balagurusamy to the Trust Office the next morning. When Balagurusamy entered Karthikeyan's room, Prof. Subramanian and C.R. Swaminathan were present.

'These gentlemen have explained all your requests, suggestions and demands to me. I wanted to talk to you personally,' said Karthikeyan.

Prof. Subramanian and Swaminathan left the room.

Karthikeyan disclosed that he had complete confidence in Balagurusamy and was ready to arrange for whatever he wanted. Balagurusamy reciprocated with the promise to make the new institute the best in the field. Thus, by the end of 1995, Balagurusamy took charge as the director of the newly established PSG Institute of Management, located just opposite the well-known PSG College of Technology campus in Coimbatore.

Balagurusamy had the quality of plunging headlong into action once he had taken up a responsibility. This was proved here also. With the support of the PSG management, he chose a sizeable independent building on Avinashi Road for the proposed management institute. It was a five-storeyed building, which had been constructed with the financial help of the central government. The faculty of the department of mathematics of the PSG College of Technology had their rooms there.

Balagurusamy instructed these departments to be shifted to other buildings. The teachers were unhappy and reluctant to move out. Balagurusamy tried to make them understand how such a move was imperative to make Karthikeyan's dream of a world-class management institute become a reality. They finally relented.

Balagurusamy worked day and night to make the classrooms, library and the offices for the various departments ready in this building. The suggestion that teachers should be given individual rooms was also accepted.

Balagurusamy had been appointed as the director, a position that had earlier only been offered to Prof. G.R. Damodaran. Some were unhappy and jealous about the position that Balagurusamy had attained in PSG. Some of his old teachers also were still working as professors at PSG Tech.

Balagurusamy was keen on placing a suitable board bearing the name of the institute on the roadside. As the board was being fixed, Poovaiah, the administrative officer of the institute, and Dr Nandagopal, assistant professor, were with Balagurusamy, standing on the other side of the road.

None who passed along Avinashi Road could miss the elegant building of the PSG Institute of Management Studies. The name board added to its dignity. The two others went back to the college remarking upon how attractive the board was.

22

Dedicated to the Core

To selves belong the loveless ones
To others the loving even to bones

—Thirukkural 72

It was a little after 2 p.m. As Balagurusamy stood on the footpath looking at the board of the new management institute, he did not notice the car that was careening fast towards him. His mind was full of his dreams for the new institute under PSG. As the car tried to overtake the lorry in front of it, it hit Balagurusamy. It was a terrible impact; he flew in the air and fell on the windshield of the car and tumbled to the road.

As the driver had stopped the car, Balagurusamy did not go under the wheels. But he was unconscious. Blood flowed from his wound and spread on the road.

A high-ranking army officer had been travelling in the car. He immediately got out of the car, took Balagurusamy and laid him on the car's back seat. People had gathered around, and some of them tried to interfere.

'It is an accident, and the police have to be informed. Nothing should be done before the police come,' one of them shouted at the officer.

'I know about all these procedures. I am an officer of the armed forces. It is more important to take the injured person to the hospital. He has to be given first aid immediately,' the officer explained and then drove straight to the PSG Hospital nearby.

Next Time, For Sure...

When Balagurusamy was admitted to the hospital after the accident, he had suffered a lot of blood loss and the doctors realized only later that there was a fracture in his right leg. During his stay at the hospital as he recovered, Balagurusamy grew friendly with Dr James Gnanadoss, the director of PSG Hospital.

'We will have to put bolts and nuts to repair the damage in the fractured leg. Or we will have to insert a metal rod through the bone. Which one should I use?' the doctor asked Balagurusamy.

'This is my first accident. I do not have any experience in the field. So, I cannot make a suggestion. But I promise you that I will give you a definite answer the next time,' Balagurusamy said patiently.

Dr Gnanadoss could not control his laughter on hearing that. Finally, a stainless steel rod was inserted to join the broken bone.

Later, as the vice-chancellor of Anna University, Balagurusamy had to take action against a private college under his purview. The chairman of the college called Balagurusamy on the phone to threaten him. Sushila attended the phone.

'Ask your husband to be careful. I will smash his leg,' the man said.

'He has already had a fracture in the right leg. It will be good if you break the other leg this time. Do not delay,' said Sushila.

The man put the phone down upon hearing these unexpected words.

This officer had attended a programme held at the Defence College at Wellington, near Ooty, and was returning in a hurry to catch a flight to Delhi, leaving at 2.20 p.m., when the accident occurred. He cancelled his journey and stayed back to see that Balagurusamy received proper medical attention at the hospital. He left for Delhi on the evening flight.

Karthikeyan, the managing trustee, and Swaminathan, the chief executive officer of PSG Group of Institutions, rushed to the hospital once they learnt about the accident. A person had seen Balagurusamy bleeding from a head injury and he immediately jumped to the conclusion that he was dead and tried to contact his wife in Hyderabad.

Fortunately, Sushila was not at home and the news could not be conveyed to her. Later, when she was informed about the accident, she was told that Balagurusamy had overcome the critical stage and was recovering.

Sushila rushed to Coimbatore the next day.

Balagurusamy had to be shifted to KMCH Hospital as PSG Hospital had no facility for scanning. The doctors had only seen the loss of blood and had failed to notice that his right leg had been fractured. It was only when Dr Gnanados conducted a thorough examination that this was diagnosed. Dr Jayakumar, the surgeon, also joined Dr Gnanados to offer expert treatment to Balagurusamy. It took two months for him to get back to normalcy. And very soon, he was back at his work with renewed energy.

Although a house and car were promised by Karthikeyan, they were made available only after six months. During that time, Balagurusamy stayed in the PSG guest house.

Balagurusamy was undergoing treatment after the accident when the selection of the first batch of MBA students was underway. From the hospital, he coordinated the entrance examination and the preparation of the rank list. He interviewed candidates while in a wheelchair. As he had followed strict procedures for the selection of students and the handling of classes by the faculty, it was possible to maintain a high level in the standard of education.

FOCUS ON NEW ECONOMIC MODELS

As a new wave of development came to India by 1991 with globalization, liberalization and privatization, there was an urgent need for new courses to prepare the youth to take up the challenges of the emerging world. Balagurusamy initiated an innovative two-year Master's Programme in International Business (MPIB), which was considered to be the best in the country. As this course was not offered anywhere else, it was announced beforehand that PSG would be issuing the certificates for this course. All the students who studied in the first batch of MPIB distinguished themselves in various fields.

Balagurusamy saw his colleagues at the management institute as his friends. Any of them could approach him and discuss any matter in detail. He made it a habit to have lunch with them on all working days. He would arrange dinner for all of them once in a semester, at his own expense. They would also go on a trip somewhere, at least once a year. He would bear the cost of the trip as well. This enabled him to win the love and respect of all those who were working at the institute.

While he was director of the PSG Institute of Management, Balagurusamy was responsible for entering into a memorandum of understanding (MoU) with the Indian Institute of Foreign Trade, an autonomous institution under the central government and the University of Toledo, USA. This gave the students at the PSG Institute a chance to acquire management training of international standards. G.R. Karthikeyan, managing trustee of the PSG Group, stood by Balagurusamy and gave him all the support that he needed.

Balagurusamy started four unique one-year postgraduate diploma courses in the PSG Institute of Management to meet the emerging needs of the market: PG Diploma in Advertising and Communications, PG Diploma in Financial Management, PG Diploma in Sales and Marketing, and PG Diploma in Hospital Management. These programmes became very popular soon as students who studied these courses got lucrative jobs.

YOGA AND ETHICS FOR MANAGERS

Balagurusamy had a great interest in yoga. He believed that practicing yoga could provide one mental and physical strength, and he extended this practice to the management executives. So, he introduced yoga into the MBA and MPIB course curriculum at the PSG Institute of Management and made it mandatory to receive the degree.

Experts opine that fine arts can be divided into 64 sections. Based on this, Balagurusamy divided the different steps in yoga into 64 parts with 16 of them to be done in each semester. In the beginning, both the teachers and the students were reluctant to practise it. But Balagurusamy managed to convince them about its value. Later, many came forward to declare this an excellent initiative. It was the first time in India that such an initiative had been taken in an institute of management.

Another initiative that Balagurusamy undertook was to ensure the cultivation of honesty and discipline in business management. With this in view, he introduced 'Ethics in Business Management' as one of the subjects in the syllabus. This, too, was another first in India.

Through the constant effort to bring in improvements in the curriculum and the management of the institute, Balagurusamy succeeded in keeping its standard at a high level.

Thus, he delivered on the promise that he had given the managing trustee, G.R. Karthikeyan, that the PSG Institute of Management would attain international prestige.

The Challenge and the Outcome

The book, Programming in ANSI C, written by Balagurusamy had become very famous. One day, Balagurusamy was invited to inaugurate a seminar on 'Object-Oriented Programming' in the Tamil Nadu College of Engineering near Coimbatore. He went for the inauguration early in the morning and then returned to PSG. On reaching home in the evening, Sushila asked him, 'Where did you go in the morning in a hurry?' He told her about the seminar which he had inaugurated.

'Very good. Now, here is a question. If you give me the correct answer, you will get your evening snacks and coffee.' Sushila was ready with the tricky question. 'What is Java?'

'Isn't that an island near Sumatra?' Balagurusamy asked.

'No. Your answer is wrong, and you have lost your coffee today.' Sushila smiled and gave him the day's newspaper.

'Read this,' she said, laughing. 'Java is an object-oriented computer language. Did you go to inaugurate the seminar without knowing this?'

Although Balagurusamy felt a bit embarrassed, Sushila's words ignited a new enthusiasm in his mind.

Balagurusamy said to Sushila, 'I will take this as a challenge. Within six months, I will develop a new book on Java.'

And he was true to his word. Within six months, his new book on Java was ready.

Balagurusamy's mathematics teacher, Prof. N.K. Venkatasubramanian, who had long ago persuaded and encouraged Balagurusamy to continue his studies when he had decided to quit PSG Polytechnic, retired from the PSG College of Technology in 1996. Balagurusamy did not allow him to leave after retirement; he appointed him as Professor Emeritus in the PSG Institute of Management. Prof. Venkatasubramanian had once expressed his desire to know more about the computer language Java. Balagurusamy was, at the time, writing the book on Java.

'I am now writing a book on Java. As I finish each chapter, I will give it to you. You can understand everything about Java,' Balagurusamy told him.

The doubts that Prof. Venkatasubramanian had when studying Java using Balagurusamy's book and some of his opinions and suggestions helped Balagurusamy polish his book; it lacked nothing. Balagurusamy did not forget to mention his indebtedness to Prof. Venkatasubramanian in the acknowledgement section of that book.

The last word in the affairs of all PSG institutions rested with the PSG Trust. G.R. Karthikeyan, the managing trustee, had personally taken an interest in bringing Balagurusamy in as the director of the PSG Institute of Management. The management of the trust changed hands once every five years. Karthikeyan's term ended in November 2000, and a new managing trustee took charge. Balagurusamy sought an appointment to meet him in person, but it was not granted for some reason. Balagurusamy felt disappointed at this, especially as many of the promises Karthikeyan had made had not been fulfilled before his departure.

With a troubled heart, Balagurusamy resigned from the post of the director of the PSG Institute of Management on 20 November 2000. He had done so without waiting to get another job. He was not ready to ask anyone for anything. He decided to spend the rest of his life writing books and in social service. He took a house on rent at Sai Baba Colony in Coimbatore with this intention.

23
A New Enterprise in Bangalore

To meet with joy and part with thought
of learned men, this is the art.

—Thirukkural 394

During his stay in Coimbatore after leaving PSG, Balagurusamy kept himself busy preparing material for his books and involving himself in social work. In the mornings, he worked on his writing and he would engage himself in social work in the afternoons. Sushila was in charge of the EBG Foundation established in Hyderabad. Balagurusamy decided that he should devote more attention to the social service activities of the EBG Foundation.

In January 2001, Prime Minister A.B. Vajpayee and Pramod Mahajan, minister for communications and information technology, came to Coimbatore to participate in a conference on Information Technology. Balagurusamy was one of the speakers at that conference.

In his speech, Balagurusamy put forward two important suggestions. While he was happy that India was leading in the production of software engineers, he pointed out how computer experts and other technologists were shifting base to foreign countries. This needed to be stopped. He wanted the central and state governments to have adequate plans to utilize the services of these experts for the social and financial development of the country. His second suggestion was related to hardware manufacturing. India was leading in the production of computer hardware at one time but had then fallen behind. Special attention needed to be paid to bring India to the forefront again in hardware production. This would not only create more employment opportunities, but also result in saving a considerable amount of foreign exchange.

Both the suggestions put forth by Balagurusamy were taken seriously. S. Gurumurthy, a well-known auditor and columnist, who is now the editor of *Thuglak*, a Tamil weekly, and C.P. Radhakrishnan, a prominent Bharatiya Janata Party (BJP) leader, were also participating in the seminar. Balagurusamy was well known among the members of the central ministries as an efficient educationist. As many of the local leaders of the ruling BJP party were friends of Balagurusamy, they invited him to join the party. But Balagurusamy was not interested in politics.

Balagurusamy was in the habit of expressing his affinity to political parties based on the stance they had taken, their work, and their ability to perform. Balagurusamy had great respect for Vajpayee as he saw the progress achieved by his government in areas like information technology, science and technology, infrastructure development and education. On this basis alone, some of his friends had invited him to join the ruling party. When Balagurusamy met Vajpayee personally during the conference, someone tried to persuade him to join the party there as well. But he did not show much interest and kept himself aloof.

FOUNDATION FOR THE NEW UNIVERSITY

In March 2001, a gentleman named Patanjali came to Coimbatore to meet Balagurusamy and discuss certain matters. Patanjali knew Balagurusamy as he had been involved in working for the educational institutions under the Chinmaya Mission at Coimbatore.

'Mr R. Chenraj Jain, who runs some educational institutions in Bangalore, knows you well. He has read your books and has great respect for you. I have come to meet you as he instructed,' the visitor said. 'Chenraj Jain, a magnanimous personality, wants to do more in education and wants your help in accomplishing that. He is planning to start a university. He would like you to guide him in establishing and running the university. With this request, I have come to see you,' he revealed to Balagurusamy.

Balagurusamy was not very eager to accept the offer.

'I have decided to devote my time entirely to the writing of books

CONDUCT CERTIFICATE.

Board High School,
Aravakurichi,
Tiruchirapalli District

13.6.1962.

This is to certify that ..E. Balagurusamy.......... has studied from VIII to X during the years ..1959-62......
He has passed /failed /discontinued in Tenth Form/Standard
During the period of his/her study his/her conduct and character
have been ..good..

His attendance is ..Very regular.... Holds the first rank in school deserves encouragement

Thomas hour Susamy
Headmaster

Aravakurichi,
13-6-1962.

The conduct certificate written by the headmaster of Aravakurichi High School, Tiruchirappalli, Tamil Nadu, after E. Balagurusamy secured the first rank in school

Prof. E. Balagurusamy (left) receiving an award from Prof. M. Anandakrishnan (right), former vice-chancellor of Anna University, in the presence of G.R. Karthikeyan, managing trustee of PSG Group of Institutions

Prof. E. Balagurusamy seen in the company of G.K. Devarajulu, founder of LMW Group, and G.R. Govindarajulu, former managing trustee of PSG Group of Institutions, in Coimbatore, Tamil Nadu

(Left to right) Prof. E. Balagurusamy with C.P. Radhakrishnan, former state president of BJP in Tamil Nadu, Pon Radhakrishnan, former union minister and Atal Bihari Vajpayee, former prime minister of India

Prof. E. Balagurusamy (left) with Arun Nigavekar, former chairman of the University Grants Commission and former vice-chancellor of Savitribai Phule Pune University

Members of the State Planning Commission with J. Jayalalithaa, former chief minister of Tamil Nadu

Experts, including Prof. E. Balagurusamy, briefing N.T. Rama Rao, former chief minister of Andhra Pradesh, about the usage of computers for medical and health services

(From left to right) Prof. E. Balagurusamy, J. Jayalalithaa, former chief minister of Tamil Nadu, L.K. Advani, former deputy prime minister of India and Ravi Shankar Prasad, former union minister, launching the first community radio at Anna University

Prof. E. Balagurusamy (left) with the former Prime Minister of India, Dr Manmohan Singh, after joining the Union Public Service Commission as a member

Prof. Sushila Balagurusamy receiving an award from M. Veerappa Moily, former chief minister of Karnataka

Prof. E. Balagurusamy with veteran film actors Narayanan Vijayaraj Alagarswami, popularly known as Vijayakanth, and Kamal Haasan

Prof. E. Balagurusamy with L.K. Advani, former deputy prime minister of India

Prof. E. Balagurusamy (first from left) with L.K. Advani (middle-right), former deputy prime minister of India

Prof. E. Balagurusamy (first from left) with C.P. Radhakrishnan (second from left), governor of Jharkhand, at Raj Bhavan in Ranchi on International Tribal Day

Prof. E. Balagurusamy (first from left) receiving a memento at the Indian Computing Congress in Hyderabad

Prof. E. Balagurusamy (right) presenting his book on C++ to Pratibha Patil, former president of India

Prof. E. Balagurusamy (centre) at an international conference in Hyderabad

Prof. E. Balagurusamy (second from left) at an event organized by the EBG Foundation to felicitate teachers and distribute IT books to government schools in Tamil Nadu

Prof. E. Balagurusamy (first from left) at an international conference on artificial intelligence in Hyderabad

Prof. Sushila Balagurusamy (first from left) and Prof. E. Balagurusamy (first from right) with Dr V. Krishnamurthy, former chariman of the National Manufacturing Competitiveness Council

Prof. E. Balagurusamy seen standing behind N. Janardhana Reddy, former chief minister of Andhra Pradesh, as the latter greets officials

(From left to right) Prof. E. Balagurusamy with R. Rajamani, former secretary to the Government of India in the Department of Electronics, and T.L. Sankar, former principal finance secretary to the Government of Andhra Pradesh

Prof. E. Balagurusamy (first from left) being awarded the 'For the Sake of Honour Award' by Ranjana Kumar, former chairperson and managing director of Indian Bank

(From left to right) Prof. E. Balagurusamy with N.T. Rama Rao, former chief minister of Andhra Pradesh, and Prof. M.G.K. Menon at an event in Hyderabad

Murli Manohar Joshi (left), veteran leader of the Bharatiya Janata Party, discussing some of the issues related to deemed universities in India with Prof. E. Balagurusamy

(From right to left) Prof. E. Balagurusamy with Surjit Singh Barnala, former governor of Tamil Nadu, and eminent geneticist and agricultural scientist Prof. M.S. Swaminathan

(From left to right) Prof. E. Balagurusamy with former Union Minister Dr B.B. Ramaiah, G.R. Karthikeyan, Trustee, PSG Institutions and P.L. Sanjeeva Reddy, Director, Indian Institute of Public Administration

Prof. E. Balagurusamy (first from right) with Dr Verghese Kurien (middle), the Indian entrepreneur who engineered the 'white revolution' in the dairy sector in India

Nermayin Payanam, a book in Tamil about the extraordinary life of Prof. E. Balagurusamy, was released by Nirmala Sitharaman, Union Minister of Finance and Corporate Affairs

Prof. E. Balagurusamy (second from left) with former Union Minister Pramod Mahajan (third from left)

(From left to right) Dr A.P.J. Abdul Kalam, former president of India, Prof. E. Balagurusamy and Prof. Sushila Balagurusamy during the oath-taking ceremony of President Kalam at Rashtrapati Bhavan, New Delhi

Prof. E. Balagurusamy (right) with K. Rosaiah, former chief minister of Andhra Pradesh

Prof. E. Balagurusamy (first from left) receiving the 'Lifetime Achievement Award' from EMC Corporation, USA

Prof. E. Balagurusamy (right) being administered into office by Gurbachan Jagat, former chairman of the Union Public Service Commission

Prof. E. Balagurusamy (left) with R.N. Ravi, governor of Tamil Nadu

Prof. E. Balagurusamy (third from left) with Rajeev Chandrasekhar (second from left), Minister of State for Electronics and Information Technology, at St. Teresa's College, Ernakulam, Kerala

Prof. E. Balagurusamy with Union Minister of State Ashwini Kumar Choubey

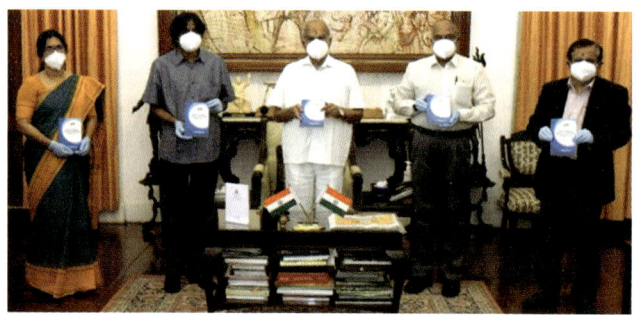

Prof. E. Balagurusamy (second from left) seen with senior government officials and fellow experts during the release of National Education Policy 2020 at Raj Bhavan, Chennai, Tamil Nadu

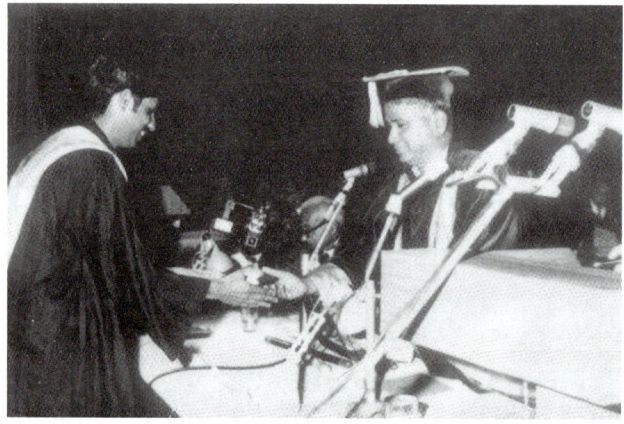

E. Balagurusamy (left) being rewarded for securing the first rank in ME (Electrical) at the Indian Institute of Technology, Roorkee

Prof. E. Balagurusamy (first from left) with his elder brother E. Perumal (second from left) in Andipattikottai village of Karur district in Tamil Nadu

*Ram Nath Kovind (right), former president of India,
with Prof. E. Balagurusamy*

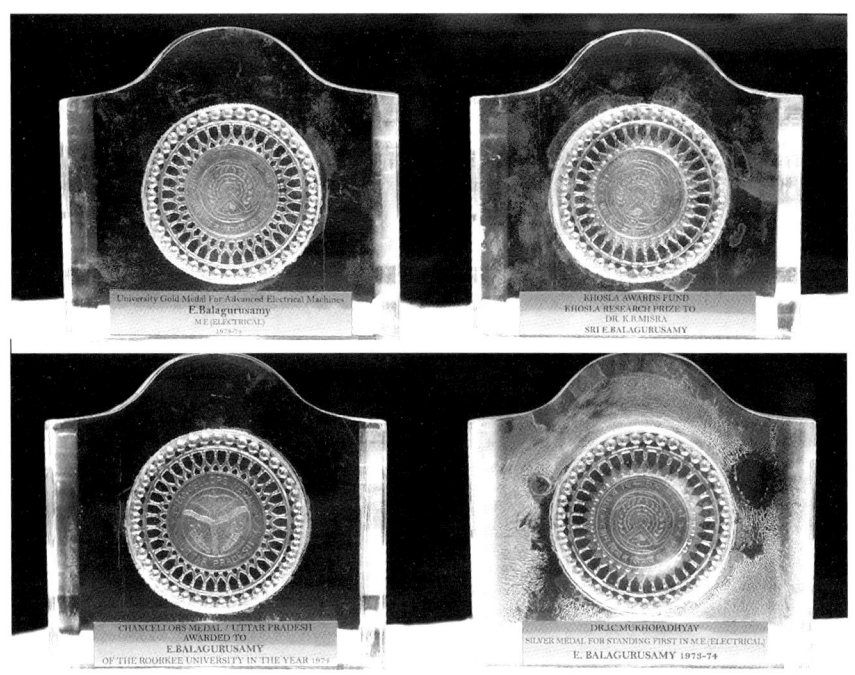

The medals won by E. Balugurusamy at the Indian Institute of Technology, Roorkee, for exceptional academic performance

The 'Lifetime Achievement Award' won by Prof. E. Balagurusamy for his contributions as a scientist

and the management of the EBG Foundation. I do not want to work under anybody any more. I have no desire to work for money. I appreciate Chenraj's desire to do something in the field of education, but I know nothing about the organizations under Chenraj Jain. I will first have to see those institutions and know more about them. Only then can I decide if I want to work for him,' Balagurusamy informed Patanjali with due respect.

Chenraj Jain appreciated his honesty, and after Balagurusamy had spoken with him Jain agreed to all the suggestions that had been raised during the discussion. He sent plane tickets and made all other travel arrangements for him to reach Bangalore. Jain had an arts college in the city and an international school outside the city, near Kanakapura. As soon as they met, Balagurusamy talked in detail about his views. Jain then took Balagurusamy to the Jain International Residential School (JIRS) run by him. It was an institution spread over 150 acres of land with excellent infrastructure and a very high standard of education; the fee was also very high, in keeping with the high standards. Only students from affluent families could afford to get admission there. But none of this attracted Balagurusamy.

'You have seen this school. There is another school too. I would like you to see that now,' said Jain.

The students who attended the second school they visited, Jain Vidyaniketan (JVN), came from financially backward families. All the facilities that were given to the wealthy students of JIRS were made available to the students here, too, including food, clothing, good academic resources and facilities for sports and other extracurricular activities. No fee was collected from the students here, except for a token fee of one rupee. Buses for the students were also arranged. More than two thousand rural students studied there. These aspects attracted Balagurusamy immensely.

On that day, Jain and Balagurusamy joined the students of JVN for lunch.

'The Jain community is generally affluent. I take money from them in JIRS and use it for the poor people in JVN,' Jain said.

Balagurusamy did not have to think any more about it. 'Yes, I am with you,' he said.

Jain was delighted and asked, 'When can you join us? What should I pay you as your salary?'

'I don't have to say anything about my salary. Whatever you decide to pay me, I will accept it—even if it is one rupee. But I want a good house to live in. I have a car. So you need not provide one,' answered Balagurusamy.

As everything had been fixed, Balagurusamy reached Bangalore on 1 May 2001. On arrival, Balagurusamy was surprised to see that a new bungalow on Hundred Feet Road had been arranged for his stay. A new AC Ford car with a driver was also arranged for his use. For a few seconds, Balagurusamy's thoughts went back to the days of joining the PSG Group.

From the very first day, Chenraj and Balagurusamy engaged themselves in serious discussions about different projects; they wanted to focus primarily on the opening of an autonomous university. But Balagurusamy suggested that it would be better to start a postgraduate level science and technology institute first. Once that was well established, they could try to start a university. Jain agreed with him. So they immediately started looking for infrastructure to build the proposed institute.

Within a couple of days, Jain found a building in the sixth phase of Jayanagar in Bangalore for rent. The building had been constructed for someone starting an IT company. It was a three-storeyed building with a lot of open space. Balagurusamy approved the choice.

Within two months, all the facilities needed for an institute were created in that building. By that time, Balagurusamy had completed all academic requirements. Prof. N.V.H. Krishnan and Prof. Uday Chandra, who had joined the institute as professors, helped him formulate the curriculum for the following two postgraduate programmes.

- Master's Programme in International Business (MPIB)
- Master's Programme in Information Technology (MPIT)

The institute was named the Mahaveer Academy of Technology and Sciences (MATS) and was initially launched on 1 September 2001, with the above two programmes. Balagurusamy also created two bodies—the Governing Council with eminent administrators, and the Academic Council with renowned academicians—to oversee the functioning of MATS.

MATS grew fast as a reputed institution, maintaining high academic standards and became an autonomous university within five years.

Balagurusamy loved writing books. During the eleven months that he was engaged in building the Mahaveer Academy, he worked during the night, developing a book on a new computer language 'C#'.

24

Challenges and Achievements

*This work, by this, this man can do,
like this entrust the duty due.*

—Thirukkural 517

It was a Saturday morning. Since Saturdays were holidays at the institute, Balagurusamy was relaxed and reading newspapers in his home office. Suddenly, his mobile phone rang. 'Sir, am I speaking to Prof. Balagurusamy?' a woman's voice on the phone asked.

'Yes,' said Balagurusamy.

'I am calling from the office of the Governor of Tamil Nadu. I am the secretary to the governor. Orders have been issued appointing you as the vice-chancellor of Anna University, Chennai.'

Balagurusamy wondered whether he had heard right. 'What are you saying, Madam?' he asked anxiously.

'Yes, Sir. You have been appointed as the vice-chancellor of Anna University. You must meet the chief minister, accept the appointment orders, and take charge. We are making all the arrangements,' the woman repeated.

'I am now working as the director of a new educational institution in Bangalore. I am not interested in another job. I have also made plans to write a few more books. And, more than all that, I have never been to Anna University and I know nothing about it,' Balagurusamy said clearly.

'Sir, the governor has already signed the orders. The chief minister has been informed of the matter. You have to take charge. There is no time to think of any alternative plans. The university can't function without a vice-chancellor.' The officer, too, made her predicament clear.

Now Balagurusamy was in a dilemma. He had divided his time

between his work for the Mahaveer Academy and the writing of his books. Before he could think any further, he got another call from the office of the Chief Minister of Tamil Nadu. The secretary to the chief minister informed him that he should meet the chief minister at 4.15 p.m. on Tuesday (14 May 2002), and receive the orders appointing him as the vice-chancellor.

Though Balagurusamy had acted as advisor to the governments of Andhra Pradesh, Rajasthan and Punjab, it was Sushila who had advised him and persuaded him to accept a new job whenever the occasion arose. Now, Balagurusamy was in Bangalore engaged in the work for the Mahaveer Academy, while Sushila was in Hyderabad looking after the work of the EBG Foundation. So he informed the secretary that he would speak with his wife and tell them whether he was ready to accept the position as the vice-chancellor.

When he called Sushila she did not hesitate to advise him to meet the chief minister and accept the new responsibility. She had a particular reason to ask him to take the appointment letter directly from the chief minister.

'I am a great admirer of J. Jayalalithaa,' she said. 'She is a leader endowed with courage and self-confidence. I would love to see her in person. So please accept the job, at least to give me a chance to meet her with you,' Sushila said, agog with excitement.

Once he knew what Sushila thought about his new appointment, Balagurusamy talked to the chairman of the Mahaveer Academy, Chenraj Jain, and expressed his difficulty in leaving the new establishment suddenly.

'When a higher position is offered, you must accept it. It will be a proud moment for all of us at MATS when you become the vice-chancellor of an internationally reputed university,' Chenraj Jain said enthusiastically.

STRANGE TURN OF EVENTS

A series of events occurred before Balagurusamy was appointed as the vice-chancellor. As the term of office of Dr A. Kalanidhi, the vice-chancellor of Anna University was to end on 14 May 2002, a search committee for selecting the the new vice chancellor had been constituted with Dr S.V. Chittibabu, a former vice-chancellor of Annamalai University, as the chairman and Prof. P.B. Sundaresan, former vice-chancellor of the Madras University, and Prof. P.S. Manisundaram, a former vice-chancellor of Bharathidasan University, as its members.

Balagurusamy had not applied to be considered for the post of the vice-chancellor of Anna University. As he was away in Bangalore, he was unaware of all this happening in Chennai. Some newspapers had reported that Dr Kalanidhi would continue as the vice-chancellor. Another section of the media reported that R.M. Vasagam, a former vice-chancellor of the university, would be appointed again. It was at this juncture that the committee came to know about Balagurusamy. So they decided to include him in the list of names to be considered as well. S.V. Chttibabu, the chairman, was determined to get someone who had a clean, unblemished service record.

Chief Minister J. Jayalalithaa had heard about the work that Balagurusamy had done in bringing about technological development in Andhra Pradesh. She realized that he had vast experience in teaching and research. She also found that he had started many new ventures and led them successfully. All his contemporaries were aware of the commendable work that Balagurusamy had done in the field of education and computer science.

Jayalalithaa, while glancing through his biodata carefully, noted the work he had done at PSG College, especially how honest he was in his dealings, how efficient he was as a teacher and how good he was at producing useful books for the academic world. She felt a lot of respect for Balagurusamy and had confidence in his ability even before meeting him. So she forwarded his biodata to the search committee.

After careful consideration of all the applications, the committee submitted a list to the governor with the names of Dr A. Kalanidhi, Dr M.R. Vasakam and Dr E. Balagurusamy. Balagurusamy's wealth of experience in teaching and research, his administrative capabilities and his reputation as a leading name in the publication of academic books were taken into consideration. The fact that he was beyond the shadow of corruption and honest in all his dealings, in whichever field he had worked, added more weight to his qualifications for the job. So the governor decided to appoint him as the new vice-chancellor.

After all this, they had contacted Balagurusamy.

No Favours

When the governor issued the orders appointing Balagurusamy, he was at the Mahaveer Academy in Bangalore. At that time, he got a call from Chennai.

'Sir, I am Radhakrishnan, personal assistant to the vice-chancellor. I am glad to share that you have been appointed as the new vice-chancellor. Please accept my congratulations. Sir, I want to make arrangements for your travel and stay. I would like to know which flight I should book tickets for you to come to Chennai. And which hotel would you like to stay in?'

'Thank you for your compliments. But I have not yet taken charge as the vice-chancellor. So the university cannot spend any money for me. I will come there at my own expense and stay at some suitable hotel. I do not like to accept any hospitality or favour before joining the university,' Balagurusamy said in a firm voice.

MEETING WITH JAYALALITHAA

On 14 May 2002, Balagurusamy reached Chennai from Bangalore, while Sushila came from Hyderabad. They stayed at Hotel Residency at T Nagar. All arrangements were completed for him to be at the chief minister's residence at 4.15 p.m. that evening to accept the orders in person. There was a strict dress code to be followed by anyone who went to meet Jayalalithaa. Men had to wear a suit; Balagurusamy had never dressed that way, but he bought an outfit so as not to break protocol. The protocol officers had explained all the procedures to be followed in meeting the chief minister.

Balagurusamy asked them if he could take his wife with him when he went to meet the chief minister. The officers could not allow that as permission had been granted only for Balagurusamy to meet her. Balagurusamy felt sad as he knew how much his wife had wanted to meet the chief minister. Sushila, too, was disappointed.

Balagurusamy reached the residence of the chief minister at Poes Garden well before the appointed time. Precisely at 4.15 p.m., he was taken to a room where Jayalalithaa was seated. As soon as he entered the room, Jayalalithaa greeted him with folded hands and immediately asked, 'Didn't you bring your wife?'

'I enquired whether I could bring my wife. But I was informed that permission had been granted only for me. So I could not bring her,' Balagurusamy explained.

The chief minister talked to him about her plans and hopes for improving technical education in the state. 'My dream is to improve the quality of higher education, especially technical education. I wish to see Anna University become the best in the country. I have chosen you to lead it,' she said and shared her plan.

Balagurusamy had a special request to place before the chief minister.

'Madam,' he said, 'I will certainly put in my best efforts to improve the standard of Anna University. But I have one request. I do not want any politicians, MLAs or MPs to interfere in my work. If that happens, I will not be able to proceed with my work.'

The chief minister was impressed by the condition Balagurusamy had put forward. She said, 'None other than my secretary will contact you.'

As he was about to leave carrying the best wishes from the chief minister, Balagurusamy spoke again. 'Madam, if I ever feel that you are not happy about me or dissatisfied with my work, I will leave the job within twenty-four hours.'

As he was going back to the hotel in the car, he got a call on his mobile phone from the officials. 'Professor, why did you tell the chief minister that I told you not to come with your wife to meet her?'

'I said nothing of that sort. She asked me why I had not brought my wife and I had to explain the circumstances. I didn't complain or make it appear like it was your mistake,' Balagurusamy politely explained.

'Well, let it be so, Sir. You are invited to meet the chief minister at the secretariat with your wife at 11 a.m. tomorrow.'

Sushila was very pleased to hear that.

The next day, on 15 May 2002, Balagurusamy took charge as the vice-chancellor of Anna University at 9 a.m. As requested, at 11 a.m., he and his wife met Jayalalithaa at the secretariat. Sushila was delighted to talk to Jayalalithaa and shared with her how she had become a fan of hers. Jayalalithaa, on hearing the word 'fan', burst into laughter.

As they were driving back, Balagurusamy contemplated the various plans he would implement to bring overall development to the university.

Many challenges awaited the new vice-chancellor of Anna University.

Generosity Not Wasted, but Tasted

While he was working as the vice-chancellor of Anna University, Balagurusamy had contributed his entire salary of 36 months to the Chief Minister's Annadanam Fund in order to pay for lunch for the public in thirty-six important temples of Tamil Nadu.

Vijayalakshmy, who had been his clerk and assistant throughout the period, had sent the money to the fund every month.

'I got a chance to see the good result of my action with my own eyes once,' Vijayalakshmy remembers.

She had gone to Madurai to attend a relative's wedding, and after the ceremony, she went to the temple of Lord Muruga nearby with her family. There she saw a board which filled her heart with happiness. On it was written, 'Prof. Balagurusamy has sponsored the Annadanam (free food distribution) for today.'

'I was happy to see that his money was being utilized properly,' Vijayalakshmy said with conviction.

NO SALARY

After a week, when Balagurusamy visited Jayalalithaa at the secretariat, he put up a request. 'Madam, I do not want to take any salary for my services as the vice-chancellor. I wish to offer free educational services to my state.'

The chief minister spoke firmly. 'No. That cannot be. You have to accept the salary. Don't refuse that.'

At the time, she herself was not drawing any salary as the chief minister.

'In that case, I will donate whatever I receive as salary to your free meal scheme.' Balagurusamy was also equally determined.

The chief minister could only assent with a smile.

Sitting Next to the CM

Once, President Abdul Kalam was present at a function held at Anna University. Chief Minister Jayalalithaa presided over it. Balagurusamy was seated next to the chief minister. Balagurusamy was in the habit of keeping his legs crossed whenever he sat on a chair. Sometimes he would shake his legs too. Unknown to Balagurusamy, his foot touched the chief minister's saree many times during the meeting. It was the usual practice that all senior ministers in Jayalalithaa's cabinet attend such meetings and be seated in the first row of the audience. One of them was desperately trying to tell Balagurusamy something through gestures. But Balagurusamy did not understand what he was trying to convey.

As soon as the meeting ended, the minister rushed to Balagurusamy and said, 'Why did you sit with your legs crossed near Amma.'

'It is my habit to sit with my legs crossed at the knees. The chief minister was not bothered about it. So why should you be worried?' Balagurusamy asked with a smile.

No one in Tamil Nadu would have dared to sit near—or even be in the presence of—Jayalalithaa in that way. In fact, the chief minister had observed Balagurusamy sitting with his legs crossed many times but she had chosen to ignore it.

25
The Lion Roars at Anna University

*Courage, giving, knowledge and zeal
are four (unfailing) features (of the) royal.*

—Thirukkural 382

All the important officers of Anna University were waiting eagerly to welcome the new vice-chancellor. The registrar, the controller of examinations, the heads of various departments, directors of different centres and many others waited for Balagurusamy with bouquets and garlands. But hidden behind all these were many challenges and crises that too awaited Balagurusamy.

He must have seen and recognized these issues as he received the flowers. Balagurusamy did not doubt that his predecessors had done a good and honest job in managing the university. But he knew he may have to take up challenges that they never faced. Like a lion entering a forest of wild beasts as the king, Balagurusamy entered the portals of Anna University.

Earlier, Anna University had been functioning as a unitary university with four campuses in Chennai dedicated to education and research. When Balagurusamy assumed office as the vice-chancellor, he was surprised to know that around 250 engineering colleges in Tamil Nadu had been brought under the control of Anna University a couple of months back. He realized that he would have to take up the task of managing all these institutions and bringing strict discipline to their work.

BG and EBG

Balagurusamy, a computer specialist, is known as EBG to his close friends. Incidentally, Bill Gates, the founder of Microsoft, is known as BG. Bill Gates came to India in 2003 and visited Delhi, Bangalore and Mumbai. The chief minister of Andhra Pradesh, N. Chandrababu Naidu, and the chief minister of Karnataka, S.M. Krishna, met Bill Gates and held discussions with him in Mumbai. The chief minister of Tamil Nadu, Jayalalithaa, also wanted to meet him to discuss the possibilities of implementing some Microsoft programs. She invited Bill Gates to Chennai. But he could not come to Chennai due to lack of time. As she did not want to meet him elsewhere, she requested Prof. Balagurusamy to meet him in Delhi, representing the chief minister of Tamil Nadu.

When Balagurusamy met him, two of his assistants were with him. They were Indian experts in IT with Bill Gates. Both of them had studied at IIT Delhi. As Balagurusamy was being introduced to Bill Gates, these two men approached Bill Gates and said that they had learned from books written by Prof. Balagurusamy at IIT Delhi. Bill Gates was surprised.

Microsoft had brought out a book on Computer Language, entitled C#, in 2001, and Balagurusamy had published a book on the same subject in 2002. Bill Gates was full of appreciation for what Balagurusamy had done. Balagurusamy presented Bill Gates with a copy of his book on C# on that occasion.

Balagurusamy was well aware that the vice-chancellor was responsible for the entrance examinations and semester examinations for all the engineering colleges, the revision of the curriculum, the management of teaching-learning processes and the welfare of faculty and students. None of these aspects of the job troubled him. He was always ready to take up challenges and meet them with honesty and determination. He harboured no apprehensions about anybody or anything. This attitude made his colleagues and the students accept him with heartfelt sincerity and cooperation. As the chief minister had dreamed, Balagurusamy was determined to make Anna University an exemplary institution for higher learning.

The first interview with Balagurusamy after taking charge as the vice-chancellor was taken by Pon Dhanasekharan, the reporter who covered the education sector for *Dinamani*. He had contacted Balagurusamy on the telephone as soon as he had heard about the appointment. Balagurusamy informed him that he was in Bangalore and would be ready for an interview as soon as he reached Chennai. But Pon Dhanasekharan wanted the interview to be published in the newspaper the next day. So Balagurusamy agreed to discuss it over the phone, and it appeared in the paper the next day.

'Newspaper reporters can approach Balagurusamy on education and Anna University matters. He will be ready to verify the truth and give clarifications on any news that comes from other sources,' says Dhanasekharan. When Balagurusamy went on visits to the colleges, he would always take the newspaper reporters with him so that they could report the facts about what was happenings at these colleges.

ONLINE DISTRIBUTED COUNSELLING

Counselling for admission to the various engineering colleges under Anna University used to be held only at the Anna University campus in Chennai. All the students and their parents had to come to Chennai and it was difficult for students from faraway towns and villages to reach Chennai early enough to attend the counselling sessions. Some of the students even lost a chance to participate, and thus lost the chance to study because of the uncertainties with respect to transportation. Balagurusamy realized these difficulties and when he became the vice-chancellor, he introduced the system of Online Distributed Counselling.

Arrangements were made to have counselling sessions at Tiruchirappalli, Madurai and Coimbatore simultaneously, along with the counselling at Chennai. The students and their parents were saved from expenditure, loss of time and the difficulties of travelling such long distances. Reporters were allowed to be present during the counselling sessions held in these different places and report about them.

Balagurusamy invited reporters for dinner at a hotel near the Tiruchirappalli bus stand on one such occasion. They were all seated and ready to place orders, but none of the waiters came to them. All of them were standing together, talking loudly and pointing to the table where Balagurusamy and his guests were seated. Balagurusamy waited for some time and then called them.

'Why are you fighting among yourselves and ignoring us?' he asked them.

'Sir, we know that you are the vice-chancellor. We are all students of the engineering college near here. We work part-time here to make some money. We study the books C, C++ and Java, which are authored by you. We have great admiration and respect for you. We are arguing about who should have the privilege of serving you,' said one of them.

'Why do you have to argue about it? Each of you can serve one item on the menu. Won't that solve your problem?' Balagurusamy asked them.

'There is one thing more, Sir,' one of them said. 'We will pay the bill also. You must allow us to do that.'

'No, I cannot agree to that. You are students. You are working here to earn some money for your expenses. We are employed and draw salaries. You study well, get good jobs and then call me for dinner. I will come,' he assured them.

They were all students from the villages with limited resources. They had to study during the day and work at night to support themselves. Balagurusamy talked to them, and got to know more about them. He then spoke to the owner of the hotel, expressing his happiness at his willingness to employ the students. He wanted other establishments also to follow this gesture.

This incident in the hotel became a top news item in the papers the next day and was published with a photo. Balagurusamy never took money from the university funds, even for such official trips. He used to spend from his pocket.

SCIENCE IS THE FOUNDATION FOR ENGINEERING

After he had assumed office as the vice-chancellor, he convened the meeting of the Academic Council, which was the authority for deciding upon the syllabus and matters connected with the academics at Anna University and the colleges affiliated with it. There was a separate Board of Studies to account for each subject. The syllabus prepared by the Board of Studies had to be scrutinized and approved by the Academic Council. The Academic Council would discuss and decide upon what new lessons were to be included in the syllabus, how the lessons were to be presented, how to conduct the semester examinations, the lessons to be included in each semester and the marks to be allotted for the various lessons. This would then be presented to the syndicate, the higher authority. These were implemented only when the syndicate, too, had given its approval.

The Academic Council had taken some important decisions before Balagurusamy joined the university. One of these decisions was that engineering students needed to study physics, chemistry and mathematics only for the first semester. The second semester would be devoted entirely to the study of engineering subjects.

'When that decision was taken, there were objections that it would reduce the importance of science subjects in the study of engineering. Two main problems were connected with it. First, the reduction in the content of these subjects will affect the students adversely. Secondly, the teachers who handled these subjects in the colleges will be affected as they would have to work only for one semester and would be without any classes for six months. There are more than 250 private engineering colleges under the university. Hundreds of teachers working in these colleges will be left without a job,' said Prof. V. Murugesan, chairman of science and humanities studies, bringing the problem to the attention of the vice-chancellor.

Balagurusamy was able to absorb the importance and gravity of these problems. He cancelled the decision of the previous Academic Council limiting the study of science subjects to one semester. He issued orders restoring the system that had existed before the change.

He explained, 'Mathematics, physics and chemistry are the basic science subjects that are of great importance in applied engineering and research. Therefore, the decision to reduce the content of science subjects is not in the best interests of future engineers.'

Similarly, practical-oriented subjects like moulding, smithy and fitting had also been removed from the first-year programme. Balagurusamy brought these courses back. This decision helped hundreds of teachers in private engineering colleges retain their jobs.

The Saviour

An engineering student from a village near Madurai met Balagurusamy at his office in Chennai. He had been expelled from his college for not paying the tuition fees. The boy was worried about his future being jeopardized because of this. Balagurusamy talked with the boy and asked for all the details. Then he called the principal of the college where the boy had been studying and informed him that he was taking responsibility for the payment of the boy's fees. He asked the principal to take the boy back without asking him any questions. He even told the principal to send him a fax message after the boy had been taken back.

Balagurusamy Sir was able to find a solution for the problem faced by the students and save the livelihood of many teachers. Along with that, he was also instrumental in improving the quality of engineering education. He firmly believed that engineering education without basic lessons in science would be like a "tree without roots". The educationists and college authorities later realized the importance of the decisions taken by Balagurusamy at that time,' said Prof. Murugesan. He later became the vice-chancellor of Annamalai University at Chidambaram.

TAMIL NADU STATE LEVEL PLACEMENT PROGRAMME

Balagurusamy did much to bring new and innovative schemes for the running of Anna University, but the most revolutionary initiative was the Tamil Nadu State Level Placement Programme.

One day, early in 2003, K. Ramachandran, a senior reporter with *The Hindu* and his friend came to Balagurusamy to discuss some issues related to the placement of engineering graduates in good jobs. During the discussions, Prof. Balagurusamy told them, 'Some system has to be introduced to help outstanding students so that whichever college they may have attended, they get good jobs. Students who have attended colleges in cities like Chennai get a chance to be employed by prestigious companies like Wipro, Cognizant, TCS or Infosys. I want brilliant students from the engineering colleges in rural areas also to have a chance for such employment.'

This idea of Balagurusamy culminated in the Tamil Nadu State Level Placement Programme. This made it easier for students from all engineering colleges in the state to have a chance to get good jobs. Usually, campus interviews were held only in IIT Madras, Anna University and some A-grade colleges. Brilliant students from these institutions would be chosen for employment even before they had written the final examination. But no companies went to the colleges in the smaller towns and villages to conduct campus interviews. Balagurusamy wanted to change this system and give equal chances to all students across the state to find good jobs. Since Anna University was responsible for conducting the examinations of all engineering colleges in the state and preparing the marksheets and rank list of all the students, he knew that there were many students from colleges in rural areas who scored very good marks and high ranks in the examinations.

He called some important companies for a meeting and told their representatives, 'You can conduct written examinations and interviews to select the engineering graduates you want. But that must be done under the supervision of Anna University. We will give you the list of candidates as per your requirements in terms of marks. Let them appear for whatever tests you want them to take. You conduct the interviews. Only after you have selected them will we reveal the names of the colleges where they studied.'

With this, the doors of good employment were opened for brilliant students from small towns and villages. This was a way of ensuring social justice. The colleges, too, became more conscious of their duty to provide high quality education to their students. Balagurusamy was always at the forefront of envisaging and implementing programmes for the welfare of students from different backgrounds.

QUALITY AND ETHICS IN EDUCATION

Balagurusamy used to speak very frankly to the authorities of the private colleges about the importance of promoting quality education in the state.

'Nothing illegal should be practised in the field of education. Giving good marks to a candidate who did not study well by accepting money and allowing someone who has not registered for the examination to appear for it are grave crimes. You will be teaching the students to take shortcuts in life by doing such things. They may also follow the same path in their later life. You will have to bear the accusations for creating such unethical and ill-qualified professionals coming to occupy important places. The students who join your institutions are going there to study. You cannot discriminate against any of them, or hurt their sentiments because they are poor or rural students. You should never stand in the way of good scholars coming up in our society.'

Most of the colleges were only too willing to follow what had been suggested by Balagurusamy. But some refused to follow the directions, and some even expressed their dissent openly and suffered for it later.

Civic Duty

Balagurusamy vowed to adhere to honesty in word and deed. He took extra care to make sure that each line he wrote bore the weight of great ideas. He was always vigilant about his duties towards society. Paying income tax without fail was one of his habits. He used to get more money as royalty for his books than what he got as salary as a teacher. This was because his books had gained worldwide acceptance and appreciation.

Journalist Pon Dhanasekaran remembers reading a report in Dinamani that Balagurusamy had paid ₹28 lakh as income tax one year. Another senior journalist, Shanmugam remembers that Balagurusamy had paid ₹60 lakh as income tax. He assures that Balagurusamy had never failed to pay his income tax on time. He did not appoint any auditors; instead, he calculated the total income he got in a year and paid 33 per cent of it as income tax.

26

The Dauntless Vice-Chancellor

A brave, noble king refrains from vice,
(is) full of virtue and enterprise.

—Thirukkural 384

Once a chairman and managing trustee of one of the educational institutions under Anna University came to see Balagurusamy. He had not sought an appointment before arriving at his office. Balagurusamy invited him in after he had finished some urgent work for the day. Balagurusamy stood up to receive him with respect. But quite unexpectedly, the man fell at Balagurusamy's feet. Balagurusamy felt repulsed by this inappropriate behaviour.

'What are you doing? You shouldn't behave like this. What do you want?' Balagurusamy, who considered everybody to be equal, was shocked.

The man owned a private engineering college at Thiruvallur, near Chennai. He was begging Balagurusamy not to take any action against his college.

'Manage the affairs of the college well instead of prostrating before anyone.'

Balagurusamy sent him back with stern advice.

After he had left, Balagurusamy shared his opinion of such people with some of the professors there. He said that such people could never be trusted. And his assumption about that person proved to be true.

A few days later, the vice-chancellor's office was bustling with activity, even though it was a Sunday. Journalists and reporters from different television channels had been invited to his office that day. The students of the private college in Thiruvallur were already there with their parents. They had come with lots of complaints against the college.

The students had taken admission there with on assumption that it was a good institution affiliated with Anna University. But the college did not have enough computers for the practical classes, library books, or even enough teachers to take classes. Since the college had been declaring holidays on most working days, studies had been badly disrupted. The college had not paid the examination fees of the students to the university, so the results of the semester examinations had been withheld. The students tried to see the vice-chancellor to know why their results had been withheld. But the personal secretary to the vice-chancellor did not allow them to meet him.

Those students were subsequently suspended from their college for trying to meet the vice-chancellor. They were also asked to pay double the fee for appearing for the next examination. Thus, the college authorities kept collecting money from the students under some pretext or the other and then stopped issuing receipts for the payments.

The students had even written about this in the complaints register kept by the university, recounting the various illegal dealings of the college. There were also several complaints about how they were being tortured and humiliated by the college authorities. Those who stayed in the college hostel were allegedly being treated as if they were enslaved. There were also allegations against the chairman for immoral behaviour with the female students.

When the parents of students went to the college to enquire about these things, the chairman hired thugs to threaten and send them back. Apparently at the time of admission the parents had signed on blank stamp papers, and this was being used against them by the college authorities. As a result, the parents could not take any action. Many students had tried to leave the college in the second year of their course, but the chairman refused to give the original certificates back to them.

'If you leave my college and continue your studies somewhere else, it will be a great loss for me. So I cannot issue your transfer certificate,' the chairman had informed the students.

When the results of the examination were announced, it took many by surprise as several brilliant students had failed. Some of them alleged that the answers they had written on the paper had been scored off with ink. Apart from this, the male students also claimed that if they even spoke to female students they had to suffer threats and torture from the authorities. Though all this had been going on for some time, none of it had come to the notice of the vice-chancellor.

The reason was that the personal secretary had denied them permission to meet the vice-chancellor. Whenever the students or the parents came to the university with any complaints, the chairman heard about it immediately. However, on one occasion, the students and parents had somehow managed to overcome all these hurdles and talked to the vice-chancellor at a public meeting held in the university auditorium. Balagurusamy had then called the chairman over the phone and warned him against such activities.

He instructed him not to repeat such activities and not take any action against the students. But the chairman ignored the warnings and the instructions given by the vice-chancellor. When more complaints came from the students, Balagurusamy appointed a commission to enquire into the matter. But the chairman refused to allow the commission to enter the college and make enquiries.

However, the enquiry commission met the students and their parents to verify the allegations. They found that all the complaints were genuine. The vice-chancellor's office then issued a strict warning to the college, but that too failed to have the desired effect.

It was under such circumstances that the reporters and journalists were invited to the university to meet the students and their parents. They spoke to the newspaper and TV reporters in detail about what was going on in their college. The news was flashed on channels immediately and the papers carried detailed reports the next day.

Anna University cancelled the affiliation granted to the college. The vice-chancellor personally saw to it that all the students from that college got a chance to continue their studies in other colleges. Balagurusamy dismissed the officer who had been leaking information of whatever that happened there to the chairman. But higher authorities in the government were not ready to take any action against him.

Some of the top level officers in the Department of Education also refused to move against him.

As part of the investigation, the Collector and Superintendent of Police of Thiruvallur district met Balagurusamy and then an arrest warrant was issued against the chairman of the college under the Goondas Act.

And the college was shut down.

Despite all this, that same college was reopened as soon as Balagurusamy left the university in 2005. It was later converted into a medical college and reports of malpractices began to surface, just like before. However, there came a day when the court had to intervene and shut down the medical college. And this time, the chairman was charged with non-bailable offences and sent to jail.

MALPRACTICES IN EXAMINATIONS

On one occasion, when the semester examinations in the engineering colleges under the university were going on, Balagurusamy got a phone call while he was very busy at his office. He was informed that an ME student had been seated alone in a room in one of the colleges while writing the examination.

That was a shock to Balagurusamy. Why should one student be isolated in a separate room? Without wasting any time, he summoned the controller of examinations and the director of students' affairs and the three of them rushed to the college where this unusual practice had been reported. As had been reported over the phone, they found one student seated alone in a room with a professor helping him with the answers.

Both of them were caught red-handed.

The incident was discussed immediately among the members of the syndicate, and orders were issued to debar the student from appearing for the examination for five years and to dismiss the professor from service immediately. The college principal who was responsible for the conduct of examinations was also dismissed.

Further, the intake seats allotted to the college were cut by 25 per cent. A warning was issued to the management of the college that if any such incidents happened in future, the affiliation of the college would be revoked. Later on, Balagurusamy came to know that the student who had written the examination was the son of the chairman of that college. The person who had helped him answer the questions was a retired professor from Anna University.

The management of the college approached the high court against the actions taken by the vice-chancellor. 'The vice-chancellor has acted in the best of interests, intending to improve education. The Court cannot interfere in that,' the judge pronounced and dismissed the case. The management went on to file a complaint before the All India Council for Technical Education (AICTE) but there, too, the complaint was dismissed.

But paradoxically, that same college later became a deemed university, and the same debarred student became the pro-chancellor there. This is just an example of how pathetic the condition of higher education in the country is! Still, the fact remains that the timely and strict action taken by Balagurusamy helped improve the standard of education in many colleges and bring the colleges under better control.

WEEKEND PhDs

In another incident, the management of one of the deemed universities signed MoUs with many engineering colleges affiliated with Anna University. The matter was widely reported in the newspapers and advertisements appeared as well. The announcements stated that branches of the deemed university would be started in these colleges with weekend classes for ME, MTech and PhD.

Deemed universities did not have all the powers that government universities had. For example, they would not be able to conduct classes through distance education or part-time programmes. They did not have the authority to give affiliation to other colleges. But this deemed university had ignored all these rules while publishing the announcements.

That was against the laws applicable to universities in India. It was doubtful that the classes for ME, MTech and PhD, conducted over weekends, would have the necessary standards expected for such courses.

Balagurusamy realized the implications of such programmes. Although he had no powers to take any action against deemed universities, he could proceed to take action against the colleges that had signed MoU with the deemed university. The vice-chancellor immediately convened a meeting of the syndicate of the university. The Syndicate took a unanimous decision: 'The degrees of ME, MTech or PhD issued by the deemed university will not be recognized by the Anna University. Candidate with such qualifications will not be eligible to hold positions as lecturers under the Anna University.'

The vice-chancellor then sent a circular to all the colleges explaining the decision of the syndicate. It was made clear that any college that had entered into any understanding with any such deemed universities would lose its affiliation with Anna University.

This made all the colleges withdraw from the agreement with the deemed university. The authorities of the deemed university met the vice-chancellor to express their dissent against his action. Balagurusamy made his stand very clear to those people. 'The decision of the Syndicate has been legally implemented. A deemed university has no power to act in this way. Any college affiliated with Anna University does not have the power to conduct such classes in collaboration with any other university. I cannot approve of any action that would lower the standards of education of courses like ME, MTech and PhD.'

The management of the deemed university went to court against the vice-chancellor's decision. But the court ordered that as the colleges came under the Anna University the circular was valid. The court further said that Anna University had every right to fix the minimum qualifications for teaching positions in the university.

CLOSURE OF COLLEGES

A very prominent man managed four engineering colleges in the Kanyakumari and Tirunelveli districts of Tamil Nadu. The vice-chancellor heard of some complaints about irregularities in those colleges and how students there were being exploited. He appointed a committee to look into the matter. When the enquiry committee reached the college, the security personnel there, under directions from the chairman, closed the gates and did not allow them to enter the premises. When the members asked them to open the door, the security personnel wanted to know why they wanted to enter the college. The committee members made them understand that they were officers from Anna University, and that they had to meet the principal or the chairman. Still, the gates remained closed. They waited for some time and returned to report all this to the vice-chancellor.

Now Balagurusamy took up the responsibility himself. With the University Registrar Jayaraman and the Legal Advisor Gopinathan, he flew to Madurai and took a car to go to the college at Tirunelveli. But the gatekeepers, as usual, did not allow them to enter the college. They made it clear that they had been instructed by the chairman to not let anybody enter the college.

Balagurusamy got angry and told them to inform the authorities that it was the vice-chancellor of the university who had come there. Soon they were allowed to enter the college. Balagurusamy started talking to some officers and teachers there, trying to gather information. But they refused to speak to him, saying that he would have to meet the chairman at his residence for any information.

'We will wait here. Ask the chairman to come here,' he ordered the officers.

As he was waiting, Balagurusamy talked with some of the students. He came to know that the management had been collecting money from them intermittently under various headings. The facilities, like the library and laboratories, were inadequate in the four colleges. There were not enough teachers to conduct the classes. Some of the teachers who handled the postgraduate classes there were only graduates. Another strange practice was that the students, especially those who stayed in the hostels, were required to buy things like soaps and toothpastes manufactured by the companies owned by the chairman. The food that was available in the canteen was very bad, and even the students who stayed near the college had to pay for the college bus. Those who questioned any of these were brutally manhandled.

When an inspection was conducted in the computer lab, it was found that only the monitors (without a CPU) were kept there. Later, it was revealed that many of the other private colleges were also in a similar condition. The inspection lasted the whole day, and all the details were recorded. They left the college late at night to go to the airport and get back to Chennai.

All the details that had been gathered from the inspection of the colleges were put together as a report and placed before the syndicate. The syndicate unanimously recommended strict action against the colleges. First, the colleges were directed to rectify the shortcomings and make a report within a specified period. But as this was ignored, the vice-chancellor issued orders cancelling the affiliation of all the four colleges. Thus, the college gates which were shut before the enquiry committee remained closed forever.

A political leader and former minister, who had read about all this in the papers, came to meet the vice-chancellor to express his appreciation. He said that he was pleased that the four colleges that had followed illegal practices had been closed. Balagurusamy suspected the exhilaration of the man in the matter. 'Why are you so happy about the action taken against these colleges?' he asked him.

'I have just started a college near one of these colleges. Now that it has been closed down, more students will come to my college,' was the reply he got from the leader.

Balagurusamy did not expect such a reply from a seasoned politician. 'Don't entertain any such beliefs. It is wrong to express your happiness at what has happened to one college. Isn't it immoral to be elated at the fall of another? If any such complaints are received against your college, we will not hesitate to take appropriate action against yours as well. Make sure that your college is run well. That is how you should move forward,' Balagurusamy advised him.

The leader seemed to have understood the folly of his thoughts and he left, expressing regret at his behaviour and thanking Balagurusamy for his advice.

SURPRISE VISITS

Balagurusamy adopted various methods to keep the colleges under observation. He would take action when any complaint was received. He also took note of the reports in the newspapers of any irregularities and took appropriate measures promptly. He also conducted unannounced inspections to catch any irregular practices.

Once, when Balagurusamy was travelling from Chennai to Bangalore in a car, he just stopped and went through the gates of a college on the side of the main road. What he saw there was beyond anybody's imagination. Nothing in the way of infrastructure for a college was visible. The attendance register of the students was not properly maintained. The teachers used it at their convenience. The students complained that classes were not conducted properly. It was clear that the number of teachers appointed was insufficient to run the college. Balagurusamy's concerns about the way the college was being managed grew after talking to the principal. The principal did not have any answers for most of the questions that the vice-chancellor raised.

The teachers complained that they were not paid properly. The students complained that though fees under various headings were being taken from them, they were not given any facilities for proper study. The vice-chancellor came to know that there was an office of the college working in Chennai for students to take admissions.

Balagurusamy went to the police station nearby and explained all this to the officer there. He wanted them to take action immediately. The police examined the office in Chennai and discovered many illegal transactions. They found illicit documents, false receipts and unaccounted money in the office and took it into custody. The police officer then informed the vice-chancellor that this was a significant criminal offence and that it would be necessary to question the college authorities. Balagurusamy told them to take the necessary action immediately.

The police arrived at the residence of the chairman of the college at Anna Nagar by 7 p.m. The chairman had probably known about the possibility of a police action, and when they entered, they saw that he was immersed in the performance of a yajna, clad in ochre clothes. The police were informed that the yajna would go on till midnight. The chairman's son was standing there. When Balagurusamy was informed about what was happening, he asked the police to arrest the son and the young man was arrested under non-bailable clauses.

The following day, the man's mother and wife approached Balagurusamy, begging him to have the arrested man released.

'It is the police who have initiated the proceedings. So everything will move only as per the law. The police have evidence about the many illegal activities going on in the college. I cannot do anything about police action,' Balagurusamy informed them.

He gave strict instructions to the chairman to rectify all the irregularities committed so far and to see that such things were not repeated in future. But despite the second chance given to them, nothing changed. So the matter was brought before the syndicate. The syndicate recommended action against the college indulging in illegal activities and the trustees of the college met and decided to close down all four colleges run by them, including this one.

BOGUS COMMUNITY CERTIFICATES

As per the rules of Anna University, all documents (like marksheets, transfer certificates and community certificates) submitted by students at the time of admission had to be sent to the university for verification. During the verification, the director of students affairs found that the caste certificates submitted by students coming from different parts had been issued by the same tahsildar and had been signed on the same date. The seal appeared to be brand new. They found some further discrepancies in the names of the students recorded in the caste certificate.

On enquiry, it was found that some of the forward community students who were not eligible for admission with their low marks had tried to obtain Scheduled Caste/Scheduled Tribe (SC/ST) certificates. A simple pass in the twelfth class is enough for SC and ST students to get admission. The vice-chancellor asked the officers to examine all the credentials and make a list of the colleges that had indulged in such malpractices. He also appointed a commission to make surprise visits to these colleges for inspection. It was found that more than 1,200 students from around 25 colleges had submitted false community certificates. These colleges got more admissions and collected huge sums from these students.

The admissions of those students were cancelled, and they were not allowed to appear for examinations.

Some of the colleges had adopted strange methods of issuing community certificates. Generally, the community to which a student belonged would be entered in the transfer certificate issued by the schools upon completing the twelfth standard. To avoid producing that certificate, the colleges created a certificate to prove that the student had attended an ITI for technical training. The transfer certificate and community certificate issued from the ITI would show that they belonged to a backward community. The vice-chancellor discovered all these malpractices and brought them to the attention of Chief Minister Jayalalithaa, and with her support cancelled the affiliation of those colleges.

As the chief minister had become involved in it, Balagurusamy was able to control such practices in colleges run by political leaders to some extent. But the management of the colleges were able to get a stay order from the court against the orders of cancellation of affiliation. And Balagurusamy's term as vice-chancellor soon came to an end, thereby leaving him with no chance to complete the action he had initiated. Unfortunately, colleges had been misusing the government's reservation policy. The policy, meant to help students belonging to backward communities, could be implemented with better care after this incident.

Those who had made education into a business by providing false community certificates to students who belonged to higher castes had been active in other arts, science and law colleges. Balagurusamy exposed the work of those who took money and issued false certificates, thereby making the field of education an arena for illegal moneymaking. These activities deny the rights to students who belong to the backward communities to what they deserve as per the law.

Balagurusamy had come to know about the widespread irregularities in admissions under the management quota as well as many kinds of malpractices in the maintenance of the colleges. Therefore, he had issued a proclamation stating that students, parents and teachers could meet him in his office without an appointment and submit their complaints and grievances about any malpractices and illegal actions that had been taken by particular college authorities. He created a 'Malpractices Cell' under the chairmanship of the legal officer of the university to analyse and categorize all the representations received.

Based on the analysis, action was taken against 36 colleges that had admitted students against established norms; admission granted to those students was cancelled. Action was initiated against 25 colleges that had used false community certificates for admission. Five colleges had to face disciplinary action for creating false records to admit students against the seats reserved for non-resident Indians. A total of 20 colleges faced action for accepting students who did not have the required qualifications. All this resulted in the improvement of the standard of education provided by the private colleges.

Fraud in Library Inspection

A story of fraud was brought to light when an inspection team sent by Anna University was visiting various colleges. The availability of a certain minimum number of books in the libraries of the colleges is mandatory. Most of the colleges did not stock enough books in their libraries. When it was known that an inspection from the university was due, books from some other colleges would be brought to fill the library. Another method to evade suspicion was to approach bookstalls. They would be informed that the college was planning to buy books from them and asked to send some texts to the college for scrutiny. These books would be kept in the library at the time of inspection and be returned later on.

When Balagurusamy learned about this innovative form of fraud, he found an equally innovative method to stop it. He instructed the visiting teams to affix a college stamp on all the new books found in the library. This ended the fraud, and the colleges were forced to buy the book that they had acquired.

REGIONAL CHAIRMAN OF AICTE

Balagurusamy always took a keen interest in the welfare and development of teachers working in the university and private colleges. Many private colleges used to get teachers to sign a receipt for the actual salary and then pay them only a part of it. Balagurusamy issued orders that payment of wages should only be made through cheques, which brought an end to the exploitation of teachers.

Another difficulty faced by these teachers was that they were unable to go for higher studies or look for a better job as the management of the college where they were working would take their original certificates on appointment and keep them in their custody. Balagurusamy declared that the certificates were the private assets of each individual and that no one had the right to keep them. This, too, proved to be a blessing for the teachers.

As per the rules of the AICTE, the student-teacher ratio should be 15:1. However, some management bodies, with four or even more colleges under their control, never recruited enough teachers to maintain this ratio. When there was an inspection, teachers from one of the other colleges would be brought to the one where the inspection was taking place. The teachers were instructed to keep the badges of all four colleges with them at all times. Balagurusamy came to know about it and ordered an inspection of all the colleges under each management simultaneously. The lack of teachers was discovered, and action was initiated against them.

The Tamil Nadu government appointed a high-level enquiry committee under the chairmanship of the state chief secretary to support Balagurusamy's efforts in dealing with erring colleges. The vice-chancellor of Anna University, the chairman of the southern region of AICTE and the director of technical education were the members of this committee. As the government was also involved, the committee's working practices were very transparent and decisions were implemented without any delay.

At this time, Prof. Balagurusamy was appointed as the chairman of the southern region of the AICTE. The southern region included Andhra Pradesh, Karnataka, Kerala and Tamil Nadu. It was the first time that a working vice-chancellor had been appointed to this post. The main purpose of this regional body is to monitor the working of all engineering colleges in the region and recommend any actions to be taken against them concerning the maintenance of the quality of education, including the closure of colleges, to the AICTE, New Delhi.

27

Courage and Compassion

*Test and attest impartially,
consult and act the laws justly.*

—Thirukkural 541

One day, early in the morning, Balagurusamy went to have tea with some friends at a tea shop in Tharamani, near the Techno Parks complex in Chennai.

As they sat down, Balagurusamy told the shop owner, 'This looks very good. Is this your shop?'

'Oh! You like it, Sir?' The owner was delighted.

He thought that some high officers had come there while out for a morning walk. Balagurusamy went on asking more questions about the shop and the man answered him.

'I have taken it on rent. I don't know who owns this, Sir. All the shops here belong to the same person. One man regularly comes to collect the rent.'

The land actually belonged to Anna University. Discussions were going on about giving the land to build an IT park, named Tidal Park-2. It was brought to Balagurusamy's notice that someone had encroached upon the land. It was to gather information about it directly that Balagurusamy had gone there with some other officers, on the pretext of going for a morning walk. Suresh Kuppusamy, Estate Officer of Anna University, was with him.

COURAGE

Upon returning to his office, Balagurusamy called Suresh Kuppusamy and asked for all the documents relating to the land that belonged to Anna University at Tharamani. After examining all the papers and identifying the buildings constructed on the land that belonged to the university, Balagurusamy said, 'All these buildings are to be demolished tomorrow. We will request the director general of police for support.'

When the news of what was being planned reached the ears of some of the senior officers of the university, they approached him and said, 'Sir, it may not be wise to take any hasty action in this. This has been going on for a long time. If we take any action, they will move the court. There may be some politicians also behind it.'

But Balagurusamy was not one to be perturbed. He already had the support of the police in the matter.

What if Balagurusamy was in the Mahabharata?

When the vice-chancellor acted quickly and removed the encroachments from the land owned by the Anna University at Tharamani, one of the members of the staff of the university remarked, 'What our VC did to restore virtue is indeed the correct action. If Balagurusamy had been there at the time of the Mahabharata, he would have diplomatically got the Pandavas the land that belonged to them.'

Next morning, at 6 a.m., Balagurusamy, along with Suresh, and the police officers, went to the site and told the shopkeepers, 'You are all decent gentlemen. Do you think it is right to encroach upon government land like this? How long can you continue to work here without any ownership? So please vacate the place immediately. Bulldozers will be here in a few minutes.'

By 6.30 a.m., bulldozers arrived and brought down all the unauthorized buildings. The work was over before seven. Those who had encroached upon the land and built unauthorized structures there got orders from the court to stay the demolition. By that time, all the work had been completed. After the buildings had been demolished, a strong boundary wall was built around the property, making it secure and bringing it completely under the control of Anna University.

COMPASSION

Courage to act in this manner was one of the traits that Balagurusamy exhibited, but compassion was another trait inherent in him. He would go to any lengths to see that justice was ensured. But if he found that there was any truth in the words of those who opposed him, he would consider such grievances with compassion.

There was a staff housing complex at Kotturpuram in Chennai where some of the professors and other university staff members had been living. Some adjacent vacant places had been occupied by outsiders with the connivance of ruling party members. As politicians were involved, nobody dared to question them. Balagurusamy came to know about this. He examined the papers connected with the landownership in detail to make sure that the site belonged to Anna University. He planned everything in consultation with the estate officer of the university. After ensuring police protection for the eviction, he sent notices to those who were illegally occupying the premises to vacate the place. None of them took the notice seriously.

Soon the eviction started. Some of the leaders of the ruling party tried to stop it.

'The land that belongs to Anna University is to be used for building residential quarters for the university's employees. No one can be allowed to encroach upon it.' Balagurusamy made his stand clear. As the eviction process continued, some occupants left on their own. Some begged Balagurusamy to help them as they had nowhere else to go. He used his influence to find other houses for them. It is unlikely that anyone knew that Balagurusamy used his own money to help these people.

CONSIDERATION FOR THE ENVIRONMENT

Balagurusamy wanted the university's premises to be neat and clean as well as beautiful at all times. Once, he invited Suresh Kuppusamy, the estate officer of the university, to walk with him inside the university campus. Kuppusamy wondered why Balagurusamy had made such a request.

They walked together from the vice-chancellor's office to the gate at the boundary at Kotturpuram, a distance of almost a kilometre. As they were walking, Balagurusamy started talking.

'Suresh, don't you see how beautiful this area looks with trees and plants? But all this beauty and greenery will be lost if vehicles come to this area very often. The atmosphere is now being protected by these trees and plants, and that too will be lost.'

Suresh Kuppusamy realized the significance of what the vice-chancellor was saying.

Immediately, measures were taken to control the number of vehicles that came into the compound. Alternative arrangements were made for those students and members of the staff who came from afar to park their cars elsewhere. The vice-chancellor also started walking to the office instead of using the car. He issued strict orders that there was no need to show any special preference for anyone with respect to the new parking rules. The estate officer made frequent inspections to ensure that everyone was following the rules.

Once, one of the professors parked his vehicle in front of the mathematics department. The Estate Officer reminded him of the orders of the vice-chancellor that cars should be parked only in the allotted places.

'Who are you to control me? I have been parking here for so many years,' the professor said in a raised voice.

Most unexpectedly, Balagurusamy arrived there at that very moment.

'I come from far away, and as I am not keeping well, I can only get out of the car here,' the professor explained to Balagurusamy.

'Are you not well? Then you can take leave. Rules are the same for everyone. You must learn to follow them,' Balagurusamy replied.

The professor then had to park his car in the space allotted to him and walk back to his class.

A building committee was formed under the vice-chancellor for the upkeep of the university buildings. The head of the department of civil engineering and the director of the IT department were also members. Permission from this committee was essential for any work connected with the university's building—like repair, expansion or adding of new spaces. Balagurusamy ensured that there were more hostel facilities for the students. The new block, 'Kurinji', was constructed when he was the vice-chancellor. He was always interested in making more facilities available for the students. He dreamed of a new building to be built for the department of journalism. He was able to complete it before his term ended with the unstinted support of Prof. Nagabhushana Rao, the head of the department of structural engineering. Surjit Singh Barnala, Governor of Tamil Nadu, inaugurated the new building.

During his tenure as vice-chancellor, the path that led from the vice-chancellor's residence to the office and the quadrangle in front of the office were completed. The arch and the garden made in connection with the silver jubilee celebrations of the university revealed the attention the vice-chancellor paid to the environment and to the atmosphere of the place. He brought in grace and beauty to the place. The beautification of the university campus was achieved by taking care of the trees, cutting down waste wood and keeping the area neat and clean. All this work was done as a part of the programme to utilize vacant land in the best possible way.

28

Strong Determination

*Weigh well the end, hindrance, profit
And then pursue a fitting act*

—Thirukkural 676

At times, Balagurusamy was like a whirlwind, but at other times, he could be like a gentle breeze. It all depended upon the occasion and the circumstances. None could know what he was planning to do, but all could be sure of one thing: whatever he did would only lead to the betterment of the world of education and the welfare of students.

Senior journalist D. Suresh Kumar remembers such an occasion well.

'It was New Year's day in 2003. I got an opportunity to meet Murali Manohar Joshi, the Union Minister for Human Resource Development, at Puducherry. I could record the interview with him as we went by car from there to Chennai. Breakfast had been arranged for the minister at the guest house of the Central Leather Research Institute (CLRI) at Adyar. The minister invited me to have breakfast with him. Balagurusamy came to meet the minister there. He was followed by his secretary, Radhakrishnan, and a priest. The priest handed the flowers and the offerings to the minister while reciting some verses. Murali Manohar Joshi received these with great reverence. I was disturbed by what the secretary to the vice-chancellor had done. But once Balagurusamy started talking, all my doubts about his intentions vanished, and I felt more respect for him.'

The Open Door

Anna University under Balagurusamy became the centre of a vast kingdom; he was the moral, virtuous and just ruler. It is said that during the rule of the Chola king, there used to be a big bell hung at the entrance of the palace. History says that if any citizen had a complaint to be placed before the king, he could ring the bell and be assured of justice. There is a story of a cow ringing the bell to obtain justice for her calf that had been crushed to death under the wheels of a chariot.

Anyone could approach the office of the vice-chancellor at Anna University with a grievance and be assured of justice. There was no difficulty in meeting the vice-chancellor, whether the visitor was a student, a parent, a teacher, an employee of the university or a journalist. But it was almost impossible for politicians and the owners of private colleges to get an appointment to meet the vice-chancellor.

'"Now, most colleges are controlled by politicians, realtors, liquor barons, sand mafias and similar others with no connection with education. The commercial attitude of these people affects the educational standards of colleges adversely. The government must take action to prevent this," Balagurusamy said to the minister.

'He further explained how the working of the deemed universities and the autonomous colleges left much to be desired. He did not hesitate to point out that some of these authorities were very close to the minister himself. The minister listened patiently to what Balagurusamy had to say and seemed surprised by how openly Balagurusamy spoke. But it was clear to him and me that Balagurusamy was interested only in improving the quality of education,' said Suresh Kumar with a sense of satisfaction. He continued.

'The general public realized how vast the extent of the vice-chancellor's area of authority and control was. They saw how someone in that position could do so much to improve the field of education—but only after Balagurusamy came to that position. One of the first things that he did upon assuming office was to introduce stricter norms for admission into the engineering colleges and to revamp the syllabus for the courses. He introduced the practice of making unannounced inspections in colleges affiliated with the university to improve the standard of the colleges and the teaching there. As this enabled him to see any lapses and irregularities on the spot, he was able to take stringent actions to bring about overall improvement.'

Unblemished Public Life

Once, his office assistant showed Balagurusamy a bundle of papers and pointed out that the vice-chancellor had travelled by air frequently. Balagurusamy scrutinized each of the papers and said with a smile, 'Though all these were for official purposes, I have not taken any money from the university. I always bear my travel expenses myself.'

Balagurusamy used the car provided by the university only for official purposes; he used to take out his car for private use. He would not even take the university driver with him and drove his car himself.

Sushila Balagurusamy used to take classes for students and teachers of Anna University in English Communication and Business Management. But the university officers vouchsafe that she did not take even a rupee as payment for them.

TRANSPARENCY FOSTERS TRUST

Balagurusamy wanted the engineering degree awarded by Anna University to be of an international standard. With this intention, he made changes in the syllabus and formed a squad to conduct lightning inspections in the colleges. Even the idea of an inspection team was new to the university. Once a new plan had got the approval of the syndicate, the people came to know about it through the media; this brought transparency to all his actions.

When the system of publishing the percentage of passes in each college in the newspapers was introduced, the people also learnt about the standard of each of them, and the students could choose the college they trusted. Such actions were a blessing for students and their parents, but many who controlled the colleges were disturbed. Some colleges were ready to rectify the defects, but others saw these actions as a threat.

BAN, BAN AND BAN

Some of the innovations that Balagurusamy introduced caught the whole nation's attention. The most significant of them was that of banning plastic on campus. The canteens on the campus served food in plastic utensils, but this was stopped. This was the first time in India that such an action had been taken. Another measure that he took was to ban mobile phones with cameras on college premises.

Many soft drink companies used to sponsor the entertainment programmes held in the university. This gave them a lot of publicity and their soft drinks could be sold at the venue during the programme. Balagurusamy also banned the sale and use of foreign soft drinks on campus as a laboratory in Delhi had published a report stating that these soft drinks contained pesticides. No one had taken it very seriously. But Balagurusamy banned the sale and use of these drinks in the campuses of Anna University and the affiliated colleges. Instead, he saw to it that there was a supply of fresh fruit juices, tender coconut water and buttermilk in the canteens. Students welcomed this move, and the practice continues on the college campuses of Anna University.

As news of the ban on foreign soft drinks at Anna University appeared in major newspapers of India, Balagurusamy's interview on the subject was telecast on a national television channel. This made the companies accountable and they took efforts to protect the reputation of their products; they tried to pressurize him in many ways, and when that failed, he was offered many inducements. But nothing could change his decision. The vice-chancellor promised to withdraw the ban if they proved that there were advantages that the students got from consuming those soft drinks. The men from the companies had no satisfactory answer. When everything failed, they tried to remind him of the money they had spent on the various programmes held in the university and warned him that no more sponsorships would be made available. But Balagurusamy stood his ground and told them firmly that the university did not want their subsidies any more.

Still, they did not stop their efforts to have the ban lifted. They met Chief Minister Jayalalithaa in person and voiced their complaint. But she informed them that she could do nothing in the matter as the vice-chancellor had the authority on things that happened within the campus. So the companies had to withdraw from any further attempts to lift the ban.

Balagurusamy would often visit the canteen to have lunch with the students. He did not accept any special considerations that the canteen staff tried to offer him. He would stand in the queue, take a token and get his lunch, just like the students. As the vice-chancellor was known to eat at the canteen frequently, the quality of food served was good.

'ANNA FM', A NEW MILESTONE

A community radio system was introduced for the first time in India at the university when Balagurusamy was the vice-chancellor. It was inaugurated by Deputy Prime Minister L.K. Advani on 1 February 2004. Chief Minister Jayalalithaa presided over the function. Ravi Shankar Prasad, Union Minister for Information and Broadcasting, was the guest of honour. Balagurusamy named the community radio 'Anna FM'.

Balagurusamy got the help of Dr R. Sreedhar, director of the department of media sciences at Anna University, to set up the community radio on the campus. Dr Sreedhar had been in charge of 'Jnanavani' at the IGNOU. Dr Sreedhar brought a new scheme of the central government for the establishment of a community radio at the universities to the notice of Prof. Balagurusamy. Balagurusamy expressed keen interest in establishing a community radio centre at Anna University at the earliest. Dr Sreedhar was asked to prepare a detailed report on the community radio project and request a grant from the central government.

But Dr Sreedhar knew that there was no need to get money from the university or the government for the project. What was needed was the support and cooperation of the teachers, students and university staff. Balagurusamy ensured the help of the faculty and students. That is how the 'Anna FM' community radio became a reality.

USE OF EDUSAT

Dr Sreedhar had submitted a proposal to establish a satellite television centre in the university. Accordingly, a satellite television (exclusively for educational purposes) was set up with the support of EDUSAT, the 'Educational Satellite' meant for providing connectivity to schools and colleges, and also for supporting non-formal education. This led to the system of conducting classes for all the colleges together via the satellite. Thus, Anna University became the first institution in the country to use EDUSAT to stream lectures for students of various colleges. When the satellite was launched from Sriharikota in 2004, Balagurusamy was one of the invited guests.

Many people withdraw from a project when they find that there are too many obstacles in the way. But for Balagurusamy, once a project aimed at the welfare of society had been chosen, there was no going back, whatever impediments stood in his way. He had to face many such situations when he was the vice-chancellor of Anna University.

Advani's Magnanimity

When the Deputy Prime Minister visited Anna University, some of the teachers submitted a proposal before Balagurusamy to present him with an honorary doctorate. Some of the members of the syndicate also supported the proposal.

'Anna University is mainly concerned with engineering and technology. There is nothing wrong in presenting someone who has excelled in science and engineering with a doctorate. But L.K. Advani works in the field of public service. Will it be appropriate for a technical university to present him with an honorary doctorate?' Balagurusamy wondered.

However, as the syndicate approved the proposal, Balagurusamy met Advani in his office in Delhi and requested him to accept the honorary doctorate from Anna University.

Advani, while thanking him for the kind gesture, expressed his strong opinion on the subject. 'As long as I am in a position of power and authority, it won't be proper to accept such offers. Therefore, I want to be excused from accepting such an honour.'

On hearing this news, one syndicate member commented, 'How rare are such honest political leaders today.'

29
Decisions that Change Fortunes

Knowledge is the truth of things to find
In every case of every kind

—Thirukkural 355

Thiru. K. Kamaraj was the chief minister of Tamil Nadu. A student suffering from a disease that affected his eyes had to go abroad for treatment. He needed permission from the government to go out of the country with his father. He submitted all the papers and was waiting for orders from the government. But nothing seemed to materialise. The parents were worried whether it would be possible to get their son treated before it was too late. The boy was in danger of losing his eyesight if he was not treated without delay. The matter was brought to the notice of the chief minister. He made enquiries about it immediately. The officers informed him that the issue was under consideration and it would take a few more days to complete the formalities.

'Aren't rules and regulations meant for the welfare of people? What will happen if, for an urgent matter, some regulations are waived? Get all the papers ready and see that the boy can travel without any delay,' ordered the chief minister, his anger quite apparent.

There are many such occasions when leaders in offices of power have shown that rules can be set aside if it is for a good purpose.

Balagurusamy strongly believes in the mandate: 'Never hesitate to break the rules if it can do anything good for the people.' He says that, too often, rules are impediments to innovation.

Balagurusamy had faced many situations in his life where rules had to be broken. He had taken decisions without relying too much on the written rules when he felt that the cause warranted such an action. But no selfish motives prompted him.

ENCOURAGE TALENT

One morning, in June 2003, a gentleman from Tirunelveli, Tamil Nadu, came to the university to meet Prof. Balagurusamy. He first introduced himself as Subramanian, a chartered accountant, and said, 'My son, Chandrasekhar, is eleven years old and has just completed the sixth standard with good marks. He is a very brilliant boy with extraordinary talents. Sir, I would like to seek your blessings and advice on his future education. We learned that you support and encourage such talented boys and girls.'

Balagurusamy was delighted to hear about the boy and told him that he would need to know more about the boy's interests and aptitudes before providing any advice. Subramanian responded immediately and said that boy was keen to study computer engineering and wanted to know if there was any possibility of admitting him to Anna University.

Balagurusamy was taken aback momentarily, but he recovered swiftly and told him that he was convinced of the extraordinary ability of the boy, but he was not sure whether it would be possible to admit a student to an engineering degree course when he had not taken the twelfth standard examination. Although he respected and appreciated knowledge and ability in anyone, he would have to see if there would be any legal impediments and, if so, whether there were ways to overcome them.

On scrutiny of some of the boy's certificates, it was clear that he possessed specific special skills in computer-related areas. When he was nine years old, the boy participated in a test conducted by Microsoft and cleared the Microsoft Certified Solution Expert (MCSE) examination with high marks. Some of his achievements had been reported in the newspapers.

After talking with the boy, Balagurusamy constituted a committee of the heads of the departments of mathematics, physics and computer science at the university to examine the boy's ability and knowledge. The expert committee subjected the boy to many tests to evaluate the depth of his understanding and submitted a unanimous decision that he was qualified to pursue a graduate course of study in engineering. The report was submitted before the syndicate. The syndicate studied and discussed the committee's report in detail and decided to leave it to the vice-chancellor to take the final decision.

Based on his past credentials, the recommendation of the expert committee and the syndicate's decision, Balagurusamy declared that the boy was eligible for admission to a graduate course in engineering. As he made this decision, he remembered how he too had been in such a position in his boyhood.

'You are a brilliant boy. You should study at Guindy Campus, Anna University, under my supervision,' he told the boy.

'Sir, we live in Tirunelveli. It would be more convenient to study in one of the colleges near our city,' replied both the father and the son.

Though Balagurusamy tried to convince them in many ways, the boy stuck to his decision. Balagurusamy was surprised to see how the boy stood firm on his own choices. So he decided to admit him to the Arulmigu Kalasalingam College of Engineering at Srivilliputhur. Balagurusamy told Prof. C. Thangaraj, the principal of the college at that time, about Chandrasekhar and expressed his desire that he should study under an eminent teacher like Thangaraj.

Chandrasekhar thus joined Kalasalingam College as per the directions of the vice-chancellor to study computer science and engineering. Chandrasekhar is now a top-ranking officer with Microsoft in Hyderabad. When Chandrasekhar got married at Trivandrum, Balagurusamy and Thangaraj were present at the function.

COMPASSION ABOVE RULES

The same year saw another similar incident. This time, a brilliant girl benefited from Balagurusamy's timely and benevolent action.

Meenakshi (name changed) was differently-abled. When admission to the engineering colleges was going on, Meenakshi came to meet Balagurusamy. When she was asked to come in, Balagurusamy was surprised. She did not have legs, and her parents were carrying her. She could not sit on a chair. So the vice-chancellor made her sit on the table and asked her in a kind voice, 'What do you want?'

'I wish to join for the course in Mechanical Engineering.' Meenakshi revealed her ambitions.

Anna University offered reservations for differently-abled candidates, but none had, so far, applied for mechanical engineering. In mechanical engineering, students have to operate many machines, and to do so, they will have to stand for hours together. Hence there was a rule that any differently-abled student who applied for mechanical engineering should not be more than 30 per cent disabled. Generally, differently-abled candidates choose computer science or electronics and telecommunication. But Meenakshi wanted to study mechanical engineering, which surprised everyone.

She had scored very high marks in the twelfth standard. But the medical board certified that only 40 per cent of her body was abled, and hence she could not be admitted for the mechanical engineering course. At first, Balagurusamy advised her to pursue a course in computer science, but he was highly impressed by Meenakshi's confidence and determination. Although rules did not allow it, he directed one of the colleges to admit her to the mechanical engineering course. Balagurusamy's decisions generally never went awry, and here also his decision proved to be correct.

Meenakshi came to see Balagurusamy after the first year examination.

'Come, Meenakshi, how are your studies going on? Do you find mechanical engineering easy to pursue?' he asked.

'With your blessings, I am doing well, Sir. I will never forget you. I want to request you to do something else also for me, Sir,' said Meenakshi.

'Tell me, what can I do for you?'

'I want to participate in the athletic competitions for the differently-abled conducted by Anna University. Can you help me with that?' Meenakshi asked.

Balagurusamy agreed with all his heart. He immediately requested the director of the sports board to make the necessary arrangements for her participation. As he stood watching Meenakshi go back with a face beaming with hope, he felt elated. He saw her as an epitome of self-confidence and perseverance.

MISUSE OF COLLEGE WEBSITES

The website of Anna University provides a list of colleges affiliated with it. If anyone clicks on one of the colleges, all the details of the institution are made available. Once, a journalist visited the website to gather details about a particular college. As he opened the site, he was in for a great shock. There were many indecent photographs on it. He brought the matter to the notice of the vice-chancellor. The vice-chancellor called the head of the department of information technology of Anna University and asked him to disconnect the link to the colleges.

'Only the list of colleges affiliated with the university should appear,' he instructed. 'No need to give links.' These instructionswere carried out immediately.

'Can it be given as a news item?' the journalist then asked.

'Of course. But the action taken by the university must also be included in the news. Let it be a warning to all the colleges,' Balagurusamy said.

'You have done something good. When all the details were available on the university website, some colleges could use them to promote their institutions. Now we have put an end to it,' said the vice-chancellor in a tone of appreciation.

'How do such photos appear on the sites of colleges?' asked the journalist.

'Most of the colleges update details about their website from time to time. Some of the colleges entrust the work to private software agencies; when the colleges fail to provide new details on time and default on the payment to the private agency, the site is handed over to someone else, and they misuse it. So we have to be very careful about the private colleges,' said Balagurusamy.

FUTURISTIC VIEW

'Balagurusamy was always vigilant about maintaining the quality of technical education, making appropriate changes in the syllabus to meet the future needs of industry, taking steps to promote the potential of students and considering how it could be utilised for the betterment of the nation as a whole. So he brought in features like Outcome Based Education (OBE) and Learning Objectives (LO) years before others adopted them,' says Prof. Murugesan, who was the head of the department of chemistry when Balagurusamy was the vice-chancellor.

During academic discussions, Balagurusamy encouraged students to analyse what they had studied every day, understand the aim and importance of each lesson, and think about how it would be helpful to society. He would emphasize its importance at the various faculty meetings and at the Academic Council and the syndicate discussions. He also brought in timely changes in the selection of textbooks and the examination system. He introduced Outcome Based Teaching (OBT), a new concept, to improve teaching effectiveness.

In deciding the textbooks to be used for each subject, a list of books available in the market would be prepared first. The books would be examined by experts in the subjects and selected in consultation with the head of the department of each subject. Their decision would be placed before the Academic Council, which would then recommend three textbooks and four reference books for each subject. No one could recommend a particular book. They could not consider even the popular books (like those written by Balagurusamy on C++ or Java). Only the expert committee could make recommendations. The vice-chancellor modified the rules to make sure that the decisions taken by the expert committee would not be challenged. This made it possible to give the students textbooks that maintained a certain standard.

Balagurusamy had the habit of walking into any department without prior intimation. Once, he went to the chemistry department. 'Why are there so many constraints in (this) space when many research activities are being conducted? The rooms for faculty and the cabin of the head of the department are all so small,' he said to Prof. Murugesan, the head of the department of chemistry.

'We can only afford to buy instruments with the money allotted by the central and the state governments. There is nothing left for any other needs,' he explained. Balagurusamy got the details of some of the amenities that were needed immediately from Prof. Murugesan. Within days, the rooms for the head of the department and the other teachers were expanded.

Balagurusamy would have regular meetings with the chairpersons of the private colleges and remind them of the need to maintain the standard and the reputation of their colleges. He pointed out that teachers were the backbone of the educational process and that their welfare should always be considered. He reminded them of the detrimental effect of giving pass marks to students who did not achieve the required standards. They should, instead, be led on to the right path.

Similarly, he advised students about what they should look for while choosing a college. He wanted them to find out the percentage of passes achieved by the students in the previous years and the job opportunities they got. He also wanted them to visit the colleges to see the facilities, including the laboratories and libraries. He encouraged them to talk to the old students of the college about their experiences there. Balagurusamy would never support anything that was against the interests of the students. He was the true "Students' Vice-Chancellor."

LIMITED SOCIAL OUTING

As his books on computers were widely accepted, he continued to write more. When he was the vice-chancellor, and earlier while he was working in various capacities, he used to devote the day to official work and sit up till midnight working on his books. This schedule made it impossible for Balagurusamy and his wife to take out any time for leisure trips or foreign tours. It was only very rarely that they visited friends or relatives. Since the books were scientific and technological, utmost care had to be taken to ensure accuracy. He was cautious about this aspect. When the subject was computer programming, even a punctuation mark, like a comma or a full stop in the wrong place could change everything.

His books in English have been translated into Chinese, Spanish, Russian, Japanese and Korean languages.

'I want to write a book on computers in Tamil,' he often said when he was the vice-chancellor.

When someone asked him about the key issues to be kept in mind while writing computer programs, his response was quick and exciting. 'When developing a computer program, two things have to be ensured. The first is that the "time of execution" of the program must be minimal. The second is that it should occupy less "memory space". Time and size are of great importance,' explained Balagurusamy.

30

Synonymous with Efficiency

*His fitness for duty, (you ought to) scan,
(and) leave him to do the best he can.*

—Thirukkural 518

Preparations were afoot to conduct a conference at Anna University. Prof. Hemalatha from the mathematics department was given the charge of organizing it. She had no previous experience in such matters.

'Madam, the vice-chancellor has been making enquiries about the progress of the arrangements for the conference. Have you met him?' one of her colleagues asked Prof. Hemalatha.

Prof. Hemalatha was in a panic. Balagurusamy was particular about knowing the progress of the arrangements from time to time. In the initial stages, Ponnammal Natarajan, the director of centre for research, Anna University, and Hema Achuthan, professor of the department of geology, had been with her while making arrangements for the conference. But Ponnammal Natarajan had now gone on leave for her son's marriage.

Prof. Hemalatha remembers her experience: 'I had not got a chance to meet Prof. Balagurusamy and convey my regards when he became the vice-chancellor. I was afraid that he might be displeased with me over that. It was in such a state of mind that I went to meet him. But as soon as I saw him, all such fears left my mind, and I felt an immediate sense of respect for him. I have never seen anyone in such a high position behave in so humble a manner.'

Prof. Balagurusamy welcomed her courteously, enquiring about her name and the department in which she worked. He also enquired about the progress of the arrangements for the conference and wanted to know the detailed plans she had made for it. She felt relieved and emboldened to see his genuine interest in what she had to say. So she could give him a detailed report of what had been done so far. 'After listening intently, he gave some suggestions. After that, he did not interfere in what we were doing,' says Prof. Hemalatha.

While the preparations were going on for the conference, Dr Abdul Kalam, professor emeritus at Anna University, was elevated as the President of India. The organizers wanted to invite Dr Kalam to inaugurate the conference but could not get him. Thiru C. Ponnaiyan, minister for finance in the Tamil Nadu government, inaugurated it. The conference went well.

CENTRE FOR WOMEN EMPOWERMENT

Prof. Hemalatha also remembers how she came to be appointed as the first director of the Centre for Women Empowerment at Anna University.

'One day, some members of a cooperative society approached Prof. Balagurusamy to find out if Anna University would be able to develop a machine for the starching, drying and pressing of cotton dresses. He called the head of the department of textile technology and discussed the matter. The head of the department expressed his willingness to develop such a machine at a cost of less than ₹15,000. At that time, he asked the faculty present there about the possibility of Anna University extending technical support to the self-help groups run by women in producing and marketing specific products. After getting a positive response from them, Prof. Balagurusamy spontaneously announced a centre called Centre for Women Empowerment at the university to provide training and support to women in all walks of life.

'I was slightly apprehensive when Prof. Balagurusamy appointed me as the director of the centre. But he gave me all the necessary support and encouragement to take up the new challenge. I was able to take up many such challenges later on, thanks to his confidence in me at that time.

'When I had to visit the vice-chancellor to discuss any official matters, he would ask me to come in while he was already in a discussion with some other faculty. He would first find out what I had to discuss and then ask me to sit down. He would not say anything about it immediately. He would continue with the discussions that he had been involved in. But once he had finished, he would suggest solutions for my problem, remembering what I had told him.

'I wondered why he adopted this method and shared my queries with my colleagues. When I listened to their explanation, my respect for the vice-chancellor increased enormously. They explained how he was sure that those who came to see him would have something connected with education or Anna University to discuss with him. He wished to do this in the presence of others. If he talked with individuals in private, it might create an impression that something was being discussed secretly. He followed the same principle of talking in the presence of others even when some of the authorities of the private colleges under the university came to see him. He was sure that they would have come seeking special considerations,' Prof. Hemalatha said.

'Sometimes, when a teacher like me was in his room, he would ask us to read the note or letter brought to him. He would ask us to give him a brief idea of the contents before signing the letter and returning it. By doing this, he showed that all the university staff were equally responsible, and he had complete trust in those who worked with him. Since the vice-chancellor was signing the letter, respecting the integrity of the person who had read it, no one would carelessly deal with such things,' explained Prof. Hemalatha.

STRONG COMMITMENT

'We started a farm training programme for the women's cooperative societies of Karalapakkm village in Thiruvallur district. One of the items for which training was given was the cultivation and marketing of stevia, a sugar substitute plant. It was a three-year programme conducted with financial support from the department of biotechnology under the Government of India. The women showed a lot of enthusiasm for the training. Experts from Bangalore were in charge of the training. We had made arrangements for the sale of the product they cultivated. The Centre for Women Empowerment and the Chennai College of Sociology jointly organized the training programme. We wanted to invite the vice-chancellor to inaugurate the programme, but his secretary, Radhakrishnan, informed us that Prof. Balagurusamy was not keeping well. Though disappointed, we decided to meet the vice-chancellor to enquire about his health and then decide whom to invite for the function,' remembers Hemalatha.

'"Indeed, I am not well, but who said I will not participate in the programme? I have been advised to rest. But this is a significant occasion, and I will certainly participate in your meeting," Balagurusamy said. We were all very happy.'

'Still, he is not well, and if he feels any difficulty during the long journey, you will be responsible,' Radhakrishnan reminded the organizers.

'It was true that Balagurusamy was not keeping well. He was exhausted too. But he came for the meeting, forgetting all his difficulties, and the programme was a great success. But immediately after the meeting, he felt ill, and Prof. Arun Balakrishnan of the department of biotechnology took him to Apollo Hospital.'

Prof. Hemalatha quoted the above incident to show how, once he had committed himself to a project, Balagurusamy would keep his word despite any inconvenience to himself.

STAND BY THE NEEDY

Balagurusamy was interested in the overall development and welfare of the education system in the state. He established the Centre for Students Affairs to solve the problems of the students of Anna University as well as the Centre for Affiliated Colleges, for coordinating the working of the colleges affiliated with Anna University.

One morning, he received a letter from a college student from Dharmapuri. The contents gave a rude shock to Balagurusamy.

This student had joined a college after paying a donation. Now he had to shift to another location, and he had submitted an application asking for the return of his certificates and the money he had given as donation. But the college authorities were not willing to oblige. He had to get the certificates and the money by 26 January, otherwise, he would be in great trouble. The student ended the letter by saying that if things were not sorted out, he would commit suicide by immolating himself. Even then, there had been no positive response from the college.

Balagurusamy instructed P.R. Gopinathan, the legal officer, to intervene immediately and find a solution.

Gopinathan remembers what followed. 'It was a challenging situation. On the strength of the orders from the vice-chancellor, I asked the authorities of the college to come immediately to Anna University. Prof. Balagurusamy asked them to return the certificates and the money to the student, get a receipt, and submit it to Anna University. He made it clear that if all this was not done within forty-eight hours, the affiliation of the college would be withdrawn. He instructed me to keep the papers ready. The authorities of the college had no other option except to bow before the ultimatum given by the vice-chancellor. They immediately returned the money and the certificates and the problem was solved.'

Another incident where Balagurusamy intervened occurred at a college near Chennai. A student had paid ₹5 lakh as capitation fee for joining a college. The parents were poor, but they mortgaged their farmland to get the money. They hoped that the son would be able to repay the amount and get the land back once he completed the course and found a good job. But fate was against them. Within days of joining the college, the boy was killed in an accident. The devastated father appealed to the management of the college to get the capitation fee back. Since they had not issued any receipt for the amount they had taken, they refused to oblige. The father was in a state of hopeless despair.

Somebody advised the father to meet the vice-chancellor, explain the situation, and assured him that the vice-chancellor would certainly help. Balagurusamy listened to the father and then contacted the management of the college.

Balagurusamy said, 'We all prioritize the welfare of children. You must understand the pain of the father who has lost his son. We can only hope that such a calamity will not befall us. We can do nothing to get the boy back. You must at least help that father get back the land he had mortgaged to pay you.'

The college authorities were not willing to listen to his words. They said that it was too late to admit another student in his place and, therefore, it would be a loss for them. Balagurusamy said politely but firmly, 'It is okay. If you do not give him the money, I will give it from my pocket.'

The authorities had to bow before such a suggestion and they returned the money.

A few colleges were profiteering and used every method to collect money from the students. One such method was to manipulate the attendance register of the students.

On one occasion, the students of one of the colleges complained over the phone that though they had the required 75 per cent attendance, college authorities were not releasing their hall tickets. As a student should have 75 per cent attendance to appear for the examination, only those students who satisfied this requirement would be issued hall tickets by Anna University.

The vice-chancellor asked the controller of examinations to look into the complaint. The controller of examinations reported that the students had sufficient attendance and that their hall tickets had been sent to the college. On getting this information, Balagurusamy went to that college. When he spoke with the authorities, he was told that the students did not have sufficient attendance to appear for the examination.

'Since Anna University has issued the hall tickets after verifying the requirements, no one can stop the students from writing the examination. Let them write the examination. Their results will be published only after verifying the attendance again,' Prof. Balagurusamy said. He stood there to see that the students were allowed to write the examinations.

The chairman of the college declared that the vice-chancellor was unnecessarily interfering in the affairs of the college. The chairman even mentioned that he was related to a certain high-ranking official in the state government.

However, undeterred by all this, Balagurusamy said, 'No one will be able to prevent the students of Anna University from appearing for the examinations. You should follow the orders given by the university.'

On further examination it was found that the entries in the attendance register had been tampered with. But the attendance of the students had been properly marked in the register submitted to the university. Usually, a list of names was put up on the noticeboard stating that they did not have enough attendance to appear for the examinations. When the students enquired, they would be asked to pay a fine and get hall tickets. Those who had a deficit of 5 per cent were asked to pay ₹5,000, and it would be ₹10,000 for those who had a deficit of 10 per cent. However, in many cases, such deficits had not been reported properly.

As soon as he returned to the university, Balagurusamy issued a circular to all the colleges. He directed the colleges to refrain from stopping any student from writing the examinations if a hall ticket had been issued by the university. If any such move was brought to notice, disciplinary action, including de-affiliation, would be taken against the colleges.

This put an end to the issue of robbing and harassing the students in the name of attendance.

31

Standing Tall Before the Law

Loss and gain by cause arise,
(an) equal mind adorns the wise.

—Thirukkural 115

Balagurusamy never minced his words on any occasion. When he took action against illegal activities by the private colleges' management, he had to face many legal battles. The most important among them was a contempt of court case. Everyone was surprised to see the courage and presence of mind that Balagurusamy exhibited amid an ongoing case.

'We take action against the management of some of the private colleges with the best interests of society in mind. Everyone should understand this. Many colleges approach the courts when such action is taken and obtain orders staying the proceedings. We become helpless, and the unscrupulous colleges continue their criminal activities,' Balagurusamy said during a 'Meet the Press' programme. There were ample reasons for expressing such an opinion.

The examinations of the engineering colleges were held under the supervision of the controller of examinations of Anna University. Sufficient number of question papers for all those who were writing the examination would be sent to the colleges. A few additional papers would also be included to be used in an emergency. The principals of the colleges would act as the superintendents at their centres.

One morning, during the examination, one college requested for more question papers. The vice-chancellor decided to surprise the college with a visit. There he found that many persons not enrolled as students at the university were also writing the examination in a separate hall. As the vice-chancellor had personally verified it, orders were issued cancelling the examination held for those unauthorized students in that college. But the college authorities approached the court the same day and obtained a stay order, so the university's decision could not be implemented.

Under such circumstances, Balagurusamy had called a press conference and made the statement in answer to the questions from the journalists that 'Sometimes, courts give stay orders without going through the details of the cases.'

Most reporters understood what Dr Balagurusamy had intended to say and reported accordingly. But one reporter, without much experience in such matters, made it appear that Balagurusamy had openly criticized the court. Some private colleges that had a grievance against Balagurusamy's strict actions took advantage of this news and filed a contempt of court case against him in the Madras High Court.

Seeing that the matter was serious, the Advocate General gave some suggestions to Balagurusamy.

'If the verdict is against you, the punishment would be imprisonment for six months to one year. To escape from this punishment, you can say that you have not made such a statement or that it was a slip of the tongue or admit that what you did was wrong and beg pardon.'

But Balagurusamy was not ready to accept any of these suggestions.

'I made the statement with the best of intentions. I don't see anything wrong with that. I am not ready to apologize for a statement that I believe is true. I am willing to accept any punishment for that.' Balagurusamy stood firm in his belief.

It may be recalled that the famous writer Arundhati Roy had been imprisoned in a contempt of court case at that time. Balagurusamy, too, was prepared to accept such a punishment.

During that week, Balagurusamy happened to share the dais at a function with the Chief Justice of the Madras High Court, before whom the defamation case was pending. Privately, Balagurusamy asked the Chief Justice, 'Is there anything wrong in what I said?'

The Chief Justice replied, 'What you said may be correct, but you cannot make such a statement in public.' He also suggested something similar to what the Advocate General had said.

Prof. Balagurusamy continued to be firm in his decision. But the case did not come up for hearing. He used to tell jokingly later that he lost an opportunity to become more popular by going to jail for a good cause. Balagurusamy had to face many such cases. But as his actions were always honest and truthful, he was able to come out victorious from all of them.

HONOURING THE AUTONOMY OF COLLEGES

Some authorities of private colleges objected to the vice-chancellor inspecting their institutions. Others complained that the vice-chancellor was interfering in the working of the private colleges. But Balagurusamy's intentions were obvious. He wanted to improve the standard of engineering education and give the best educational facilities to students.

There was a student protest in one of the colleges under the management of Dr Jeppiaar, Jeppiaar Group of Institutions. The cause for this appeared to be the difference of opinion between the two sections of the administration. Based on requests from many parents, the vice-chancellor came to the college to speak with the students and find out the actual cause for the protest. He also informed the press about his visit.

'Some family members of those in the management of the college have been interfering in the affairs of the college. As a result, the chairman has removed our director, who had been managing the college very well, from that post. He should be reinstated. They should stop interfering in the working of the college.' The students shared their demands with Balagursamy.

When Jeppiaar came to know about this, he came to the place of the meeting and talked in the presence of the reporters. 'This is purely a family matter. This will not affect the working of the college or the standard of education imparted. So I request the vice-chancellor not to interfere in this matter,' he said, respectfully.

Balagurusamy appreciated his views and immediately withdrew. But he also made some enquiries with the students.

'How good are the buildings in this college?' he asked the students.

'Very good,' replied the students.

'Are your classes going well?'
'Yes, there has been no disruption.'
'Do you have enough qualified teachers for taking classes?'
'Yes, we have enough teachers with good qualifications.'
'Are you paying the regular fees?'

Uncompromising Stand

Jeppiaar, the chairman of the Jeppiaar Group of Institutions, had registered for a PhD at Anna University. The university had issued strict orders regarding marking the students' attendance if they had registered privately for PhD degrees. Many important personalities who had registered privately for PhDs expected some concessions. But Jeppiaar completed his research strictly following all the norms imposed by Dr Balagurusamy. When Balagurusamy finished his term as the vice-chancellor, Jeppiaar visited him as a matter of courtesy. He invited Balagurusamy to be an advisor to the group of educational institutions under him. He was ready to offer a few lakhs for his services, but Balagurusamy politely refused the offer. He made it clear that taking such positions for money was against his basic principles.

'Yes, only the amount decided by the government is being collected as fees. All facilities provided are also good.'

'Then you have no grounds for this agitation,' Balagurusamy said. 'You have no right to interfere in the internal affairs of the management. Go back to your classes from tomorrow.'

It was 9 p.m., and the students had not had their dinner as a part of their protest. After listening to Balagurusamy they went to the dining halls for dinner with the promise that they would attend classes the next day.

Jeppiaar thanked Balagurusamy for settling the matter so well. As per the suggestion of the vice-chancellor, the former director was reinstated to his position.

DEALING WITH POLITICIANS

The son of a senior leader of a political party approached Balagurusamy to get his son admitted for the BE course in Anna University. The student did not have the marks required for admission to the Guindy Campus of Anna University.

'I do not have the power to give a seat to this student. I can try to get a seat allotted from the chief minister's quota. But I have to get permission from the chief minister,' Balagurusamy informed him.

The politician did not want that, and he left disappointed.

MP's Ego

A top political leader with an engineering college under his management once visited Balagurusamy at Anna University. Balagurusamy knew that there had been some serious complaints against his college. The man was a bit arrogant in his behaviour before the vice-chancellor. He pointed out how Chief Minister Jayalalithaa had made him contest the elections to make him an MP.

He wanted to clarify that he had some influence on the chief minister. He felt that Balagurusamy would not dare to take action against his college in light of this information. But such things did not influence Balagurusamy.

Later, when he had to meet the chief minister, the name of this leader came up during the conversation. Balagurusamy informed Jayalalithaa about his behaviour and how he had indicated that he had some influence on the chief minister.

'Is that so? If you had told me about him earlier, I would not have chosen him to contest the elections,' said the chief minister.

On another occasion, a minister approached Balagurusamy. He gave him a piece of paper and said, 'Could you admit all these students for the engineering degree course.'

'I do not have the power to give admissions. Authorities decide these things based on the marks scored by the students. But there are some seats in the chief minister's quota. I can see if these students can be admitted through that. But I will have to get permission from the chief minister.'

He asked his office to connect him to the Chief Minister's Office. The minister jumped up from the chair and with folded hands asked him to stop.

'Please, Sir, don't do that. If Amma, as Chief Minister Jayalalithaa was addressed, comes to know about this, I will be in trouble...' said the minister, his body bathed in sweat. He left the place immediately.

It was the month of July. Interviews were going on for the selection of faculty for various positions. When Prof. Balagurusamy was about to leave his room to chair one of the interview meetings, a person entered his room and gave him a letter. Balagurusamy read the letter and, without any response, tore it into pieces. Handing the torn pieces of the letter to the man, Balagurusamy said in a stern voice, 'After attending the interview, you may hand over this to the minister who gave the recommendation letter. Don't you know that any form of canvassing is against the rules?'

The minister later expressed his regrets to Balagurusamy when he came to the university to attend a function.

32

The Tree Thanks the One Who Sowed the Seed

*That land prospers where the king is
easy to see, not harsh of words.*

—Thirukkural 386

After serving as the vice-chancellor of Anna University, Prof. Balagurusamy took up residence in Delhi as a member of the UPSC. Once, while he was visiting Chennai, he invited some of his friends to a hotel for breakfast so that he could meet all of them together. While talking to them, Balagurusamy noticed that some of the hotel staff were looking at him and talking among themselves.

'Why do they look at me like this? Am I a film star or a politician?' Balagurusamy wondered. He soon got absorbed in conversation with his friends. After a while, the men came to their table and it was evident that they wanted to talk to him.

'Any problems?' Balagurusamy asked them. 'I saw that you were observing me. Do you know me?'

One of them spoke immediately. 'Sir, I know that you were the vice-chancellor of Anna University. I have boundless gratitude to you. My son is now working in a high position in a software company. Only because of you could he achieve so much.'

'But what have I done? I have never seen you or your son before. Then how could I have helped you or your son?' Balagurusamy asked him.

'When campus interviews were held in the university and in some of the colleges in the city, our children from the villages never got a chance to get such jobs. When you were the vice-chancellor, you made arrangements for the interviews to be held for all the colleges together.' 'That is how our children got good jobs. My son and I will always remain grateful to you, Sir.' The man spoke with evident emotion. Balagurusamy understood that he was referring to the State Level Placement Programme that he had introduced in the university.

It was a wonderful moment. The tree expressed its gratitude to the one who had sowed the seed! His friends witnessed this with wonder and respect. But Balagurusamy, with his usual smile, just said, 'All credit should go to your son's knowledge and ability. I could just create an environment for it. That is all.'

If Bricks Could Speak.

The Tamil Nadu State Level Placement Programme will remain the most appreciated innovation Prof. Balagurusamy brought to Anna University. If the bricks of Anna University could speak, they would sing praises of Prof. Balagurusamy.

EASY TO BUY, EASY TO UNDERSTAND

N. Arunkumar, a student of BSc. computer science course in the late 1990s, could not afford to buy the expensive books needed for his course of study. It was at this time that less expensive books on C, C++ and Java appeared in the market. While some of the books cost more than a thousand rupees, these new arrivals were available for ₹250. It came as a blessing for students like Arunkumar. Even those students who studied in vernacular medium could understand the contents without any difficulty. The author's name printed on the cover was 'E. Balagurusamy'. Arunkumar had assumed that Balagurusamy, the author of these books, must be an Indian settled in England or America. Students like Arunkumar thanked this unknown author with heartfelt gratitude.

Balagurusamy had once explained why his books were priced so low. 'I had specifically asked the publishers to make the books available at prices that the poor students could afford. I made concessions in the royalty to be paid to me to compensate the loss that the publishers would have to face.'

After completing his education, Arunkumar became a journalist. He worked for *Chennai Online*, an online newspaper, and the *Deccan Chronicle* later. It was at that time that Dr Balagurusamy had assumed office as the vice-chancellor of Anna University. Arunkumar felt that the name of the vice-chancellor seemed familiar to him, but he did not connect it with the books he had studied. On one occasion, he went to Anna University with his colleague, Ramesh, to collect some information regarding engineering education. They met the vice-chancellor who, dressed in a simple yet elegant way, welcomed them with a smile on his face.

When Arunkumar was talking with his colleagues, he said, 'In my mind's eye, the author of the books on software that I had studied was a proud gentleman dressed formally in a suit. I was surprised to see Prof. Balagurusamy as a person who seemed to be the epitome of simplicity, humility and friendliness. He treated all journalists with the same courtesy, irrespective of the circulation of the paper they worked for. What impressed me most was his ability to keep a cool and good relationship with even those who opposed him; he listened to their opinion carefully. He then would make special effort to explain his point of view so that those who were against it came to understand it fully.'

NO SECOND TERM AS VICE-CHANCELLOR

The feeling among journalists as well as the public was that Balagurusamy would be asked to continue as the vice-chancellor when his term ended. They were sure of that as Balagurusamy was deemed trustworthy by Chief Minister Jayalalithaa. The chief minister, too, wanted him to continue.

His name was included in the list of three candidates recommended by the search committee for the post. He was described in it as an eminent personality who had brought about revolutionary changes in education, particularly technical education.

Balagurusamy personally believed that much more needed to be done at Anna University. But like a pack of jackals attacking the king of the forest to defeat him, the chairpersons of the private colleges joined hands with petty politicians and sabotaged Balagurusamy's chances.

Suggestions to the Governor

The list of names submitted to the governor for the appointment of the new vice-chancellor included the name of Balagurusamy too. On the day that the list was sent to Raj Bhavan, a Saturday, the governor was in the university to inaugurate a new building. While leaving the campus after the function, the governor, who had high regard for Balagurusamy, said to him, 'Don't go out for any function this evening. I will tell you at five about your appointment as the vice-chancellor.'

But at 6 p.m. Balagurusamy came to know that the governor had left for Mumbai on a personal matter.

The next Tuesday, after three days, Balagurusamy got a message asking him and his wife to meet the governor at Raj Bhavan at 11.30 a.m. When they met the governor at the appointed time, he told them, 'I am sorry, Balagurusamy. Due to some political reasons, I cannot appoint you as the next vice-chancellor. I am helpless.'

Balagurusamy was not unduly concerned about it as he was not looking for a second term. But he suggested that another qualified person on the list, a professor from IIT, should be appointed. But the governor did not want to do so because that would lead to questions from the media and public about why Balagurusamy had not been chosen. He felt that it would tarnish Balagurusamy's reputation.

Thus, the governor rejected the entire list and ordered a new search committee to be formed to select the next vice-chancellor.

So Dr Balagurusamy completed his three years as vice-chancellor in May 2005. After the farewell functions, some of his colleagues escorted him home. As he received them at home with due respect and love, many found their eyes filling with tears. He comforted them, saying that he would come back to Chennai even though he had left the official position.

Many of those who had worked with Balagurusamy at Anna University decided to leave once he left the post. Dr Arun Balakrishnan, the director of the department of biotechnology, was among them. This was how he explained why he decided to quit Anna University.

'Balagurusamy gave a lot of importance to original applied research. If anyone approached him with a plan for a new project, he would listen carefully to know all the details. Then he would give full freedom to the researcher to do his work. But he would always remind the research scholars that whatever they did, the outcome should be useful for the country and the common person. We should never aim to copy what is being done in Western countries. Balagurusamy was always ready to listen to those who had something against his opinion, and he was ready to change his decision if he was convinced about it. Such broad-mindedness is very rare. I do not believe that there would be another person as honest as Balagurusamy as the vice-chancellor. After working with such a great personality, it is difficult to work under anyone else. So I gave up my position at Anna University in July 2005 when the next vice-chancellor assumed office.'

Gopinathan, the legal advisor at Anna University under Balagurusamy, remembered that he had not even heard of Dr Balagurusamy when he had applied for the post.

'Balagurusamy appointed me on seeing my qualifications and legal experience in the area of higher education. He gave me complete freedom to deal with legal matters concerning the welfare of students and faculty. When he left the University, I did not feel like continuing there,' reminisces Gopinathan.

'I met Balagurusamy when the university had invited applications for the post of the director of the multimedia department. He appointed me in that post, considering my previous experience in a similar position. After he left, I did not want to continue working there,' said Dr Sreedhar, who had been working at the IGNOU before joining Anna University.

Though Balagurusamy left his service in the state, there were many institutions all over the country that were eager to have him.

33
Delhi Calls Again

*Those who are gracious, but dutiful
have the right to this earth, (which is) beautiful.*[*]

—Thirukkural 578

After leaving Anna University, Balagurusamy decided to live in Coimbatore for the rest of his life. Located on the banks of the Noyyal River, Coimbatore, also called Kovai, is variedly known as the Manchester of south India, the Knowledge City of Tamil Nadu and the poor man's Ooty. The city is home to many prestigious educational institutions and universities.

Balagurusamy bought a house there with a large garden in Vadavalli located at the foothills of Marudamalai and started living there in July 2005. Vadavalli has a pollution-free, pleasant climate all through the year and is considered to be a paradise for senior citizens.

Once he had settled down in the new house, Balagurusamy thought of revising his famous books on *ANSI C, C++* and *Java*, a task that he had not been able to undertake for the past three years. For growing areas like computer science, it was essential to revise and update the contents of books, at least every three years.

In March 2006, he was invited by the University Grants Commission (UGC), New Delhi, to take over as the chairman of the Consortium for Educational Communications (CEC), a central government organization headquartered in Delhi. CEC is established with the goal of addressing the needs of higher education in universities through the use of computers and communication technology, such as the development of e-content materials and dissemination of educational

---

[*]This couplet has been translated by P. Krishnan.

programmes through broadcast and non-broadcast modes. Apart from that, it is also responsible for coordinating the functions of the Electronic Multimedia and Research Centres (EMRCs) of different universities in the country. Balagurusamy considered the assignment an interesting as well as challenging one.

Immediately after taking charge as the Chairman of CEC, he invited Arjun Singh, the Union Minister of Human Resource Development, to inaugurate the national seminar on development and delivery of e-content materials, organized at the CEC. Vice-chancellors, directors of EMRCs and content developers from various universities participated in the seminar. During the discussions, Arjun Singh expressed special interest in improving the educational standards of the north-eastern states. As a follow-up, Balagurusamy visited EMRC centres at Pune University, Roorkee University, Calcutta University and the North Eastern Regional Institute of Science and Technology (NERIST) in Arunachal Pradesh.

When he took a tour of some of the north-eastern states in August 2006, Balagurusamy noticed that education and healthcare facilities were relatively backward in these states. He felt that it was essential to give the teachers proper training to improve the educational standard of these states. He, therefore, convened a meeting of the Ministers of Education of the north-eastern states at Itanagar, the capital of Arunachal Pradesh, to discuss their needs in the area of teacher education. He explained the importance of giving teachers some training to improve the quality of education. At that time, a question raised by the education minister of Arunachal Pradesh was astonishing.

'Which teachers do you mean? Proxy teachers or real teachers?' he asked.

'Proxy teachers? What is that?' asked Balagurusamy in surprise.

The words of the minister revealed to him a strange practice.

'In our state, teachers whom the government appoints do not take classes. They only draw the salary every month and send someone to handle the classes while running their business or doing other work. They will pay five to ten thousand rupees to those who take the classes. That is why I asked. Who should be given this training?'

What could be done when the minister himself spoke about such an illegal practice in his state? That was what saddened Balagurusamy.

Although Balagurusamy wanted to do many things to improve the quality of education through the initiatives of CEC, he could not continue for an extended period in that position.

A MEMBER OF THE UPSC

Around 3 p.m. on the 4 November that year, Balagurusamy got a call.

'I am Suresh Pachauri, Minister for Personnel in the Prime Minister's Office. You have been recommended to be made a member of the UPSC. The recommendation has been sent just now to the President for approval. Be ready to join the UPSC as a member next week.' Dr A.P.J. Abdul Kalam, a close friend of Balagurusamy, was the President at that time.

Balagurusamy was shocked to hear these words and said politely, 'Sir, thank you for the kind words. But I have not applied for such a post. I do not think I am qualified for it.'

'It is a decision taken by the central cabinet. We will get the approval of the President within twenty-four hours. I am nobody to decide on this, and my job is only to inform you.'

'I had applied for the post of the chairman of the UGC. I work in the field of education. Administration is not my subject. So how can I be a suitable candidate for this post?' Balagurusamy expressed his concerns.

'The central government has taken this decision. If you have been planning any trip outside the country, please cancel it and wait for orders. Once the orders come, you will have to take up the responsibility within a week,' the minister continued.

'But I have not applied for it,' Balagurusamy again tried to remind him.

'Yes, I know. The chairman of the UGC is equivalent to that of a secretary of the central government. A member of the UPSC is much higher than that. It is equal to the position of a state minister in the central cabinet, with powers equal to those of the judges of the Supreme Court. Many try hard to get this position. Now, this has come to you. Please don't refuse it,' said the minister.

Balagurusamy was left in a predicament.

After an hour of his conversation with the minister, one of the personal secretaries of the President, who knew Balagurusamy very well, called him. 'Rashtrapati Bhavan has received the letter recommending you as a member of the UPSC. The President is here now and he will sign the appointment order today. Congratulations.' He was exhilarated.

Balagurusamy did not know what to do. Meanwhile, one of the television channels started scrolling the news on the ticker that Prof. Balagurusamy, former vice-chancellor of Anna University, had been appointed as a member of the UPSC. Soon there was a flow of calls from friends to congratulate him. Though he told them that he had not yet got the orders and had not decided whether he should take up the responsibility, they all reminded him not to give up such a high and honourable position.

After careful consideration, persuaded by his friends and advised by Suresh Pachauri, Balagurusamy decided to take up the responsibility as soon as he got the orders.

On the same day, at 10.30 p.m., the personal secretary who had earlier called Balagurusamy told him in a disturbed voice that a gentleman from Chennai had met the President at 9.30 p.m. and handed over a letter regarding the appointment of the UPSC member. He did not reveal any further details.

One week passed, and no orders came from Rashtrapati Bhavan, as had been promised by the minister. Some of his friends suggested meeting the President in person. But Balagurusamy refused to meet Dr Abdul Kalam and plead for his approval as it went against his principles.

'I will meet him only after I have joined. I don't think it is right to do so before that,' he said.

There was further delay when it came to the President signing his papers. Meanwhile, Suresh Pachauri again called Balagurusamy, 'Professor, why haven't you joined the UPSC yet?'

'I have not got the appointment orders,' said Balagurusamy.

The minister was shocked to hear this. The President usually signed such important files within one or two days. He did not know why the delay had occurred. 'Why don't you come to Delhi? I want to talk to you in person,' he said.

'Sir, I have to come to Delhi to chair a meeting of the UGC on 7 December. I will meet you then,' said Balagurusamy.

As arranged, he met Pachauri at his residence at six on 7 December. They talked for about an hour. During their conversation, Pachauri said, 'You are my guru.'

Balagurusamy was surprised to hear this. He did not remember seeing Pachauri before.

'Yes, Sir. After completing my engineering degree from MACT, Bhopal, I did a postgraduate diploma in computer programming. Your book *BASIC Programming* was the textbook for the course. It was a simple but excellent book. I was delighted to see your biodata at the Prime Minister's office. I was happy to mention this to the Prime Minister.' The minister spoke with pride apparent on his face.

The minister immediately contacted the secretary to the Prime Minister and said, 'The approval has not been received though it was sent to Rashtrapati Bhavan more than a month back. Ask the President's secretary to send the file back if there are any objections so that we could recommend another name for the post.'

Balagurusamy took leave of the minister at about 7 p.m., satisfied that he had met such an intellectual and honest politician.

The order of appointment was received on 15 December 2006, and Balagurusamy assumed charge as a member of the UPSC on 29 December.

The Path Made Clear

Minister Suresh Pachauri later revealed how Balagurusamy had come to be considered for the UPSC even though he had not applied for it. The application that he had submitted for the chairman of the UGC was outstanding, but another person had already been chosen for that post. Pachauri had talked to Prime Minister Manmohan Singh about Balagurusamy. He had mentioned that he had studied Balagurusamy's books during his student days in engineering college. He had also told him about Balagurusamy's qualifications, integrity, ability and determination. This made the Prime Minister think that such a brilliant person would do well if he served in the UPSC.

It was as the personal choice of the Prime Minister that Balagurusamy became a member of the UPSC.

FUNCTIONS OF UPSC

Only after joining the UPSC did he understand the extent of its powers. People generally think of the UPSC as a body that selects candidates and appoints them for the IAS, the IPS and the Indian Foreign Service (IFS). They may not know that the UPSC is also responsible for the selection and appointment of officers for twenty-four other higher administrative posts, like the Indian Revenue Service (IRS), the Indian Engineering Service (IES) and the Indian Legal Service (ILS). A preliminary examination is held first, and those who qualify are allowed to appear for the main examination. Those who secure high ranks are called for an interview and those recommended after the interview are appointed in different departments according to the ranks they secure.

Apart from these higher-level administrative posts, the UPSC is also responsible for the selection of some of the middle-level posts in various central government departments.

Another vital task entrusted to the UPSC is the recommendation to promote officers in different departments under the central government. A Promotion Committee, under the chairmanship of a UPSC member, considers the details of the experience and the annual confidential report (ACR) of the candidates submitted by the departments and recommend promotions as per the applicable reservation rules.

The senior administrative officers in the state service who are eligible to be promoted to IAS and IPS cadres are selected by the UPSC. This practice, referred to as conferment, is done after holding an interview. The committee that selects officers for conferment comprises a member of the UPSC, two joint secretaries from the central service and the chief secretary and the director general of police of the state concerned. The state government suggests the names of five officers for each post. The UPSC then considers their qualifications, experience, ability and confidential reports and holds an interview to select the candidate.

Balagurusamy had visited many state capitals, including Patna, Ahmedabad, Srinagar, Bangalore, Bhopal, Thiruvananthapuram and Ranchi, conducting such interviews.

The most challenging job that the UPSC has to perform is connected with the disciplinary cases of IAS officers. The UPSC has to decide the disciplinary action that needs to be taken against an erring officer. The UPSC does not examine the officer directly. They study the report of the enquiry held by the government and all other relevant documents and then recommend suitable punishment in the form of a judgement. This is what makes the power of the members of the UPSC equal to that of the judges of the Supreme Court.

In the four years that he was a member of the UPSC, Balagurusamy had written judgements for more than 75 disciplinary cases, the majority of them being corruption cases. Some of these officers were removed from their position. In some instances, increments were withheld as punishment. If the accused had retired from service, the punishment would involve reduction or cancellation of pension. In some cases where enough evidence could not be gathered, the accused were let off without any penalties.

No To Recommendations

The members of the UPSC would never consider recommendations made by those in power, including ministers. Balagurusamy had to reject a proposal once. When Balagurusamy was in Kolkata on official duty, a central minister contacted him on the phone. He wanted Balagurusamy to intervene in an interview of one of the officers appearing for the IAS selection on 31 December and help him.

'We do not accept phone calls like this from officers in the government or from ministers. You are not supposed to make recommendations like this,' said Balagurusamy.

On another occasion, a senior central minister called him to recommend a person to be appointed as the company registrar. He added that this officer was quite capable and reminded him that we should encourage such people.

'Sir, don't you know that you are not supposed to speak to the members of UPSC. Such recommendations are not allowed. Remember, your words are being recorded by our office,' Balagurusamy informed him politely.

Immediately the minister put the phone down.

OFFER OF GOVERNORSHIP

Balagurusamy came to Thiruvananthapuram on 30 December 2009, to consider the matter of the elevation of a senior state officer to the IAS cadre. He got a call from a leader of a political party who wanted to meet him to discuss an important matter. Balagurusamy informed him that he was in Thiruvananthapuram but would be in Chennai on his way back to Delhi. He could meet him there.

On 1 January 2010, the leader came to meet Balagurusamy at the hotel where he was staying. They talked about various matters before the leader got to the important point.

'Your name has been included in the list of those considered for appointment as lieutenant governor in a Union Territory. Discussions are being held about it in the Prime Minister's Office,' he informed Balagurusamy.

'How did my name come to be included in this list?' asked Balagurusamy out of curiosity.

'You are honest, impartial and bold. Moreover, you are already a member of a constitutional body. If people like you are appointed, it will be an honourable achievement for the government. It is better to appoint well-known experts like you than political leaders,' the leader explained.

'Good. If they want to do so, let them appoint me. The Prime Minister's Office has all the details about me. The Prime Minister knows me personally. Why should there be a mediator for this?' Balagurusamy asked.

'That is not the problem, Sir. The final decision has to be taken by a top political leader. He wants some money to make the decision,' the man explained the reason for his meeting.

Balagurusamy had never imagined that there were leaders who demanded money, even for the appointment of governors! It was well known that politicians demanded money to allot prestigious posts, but he had never experienced such a situation.

He did not reveal the shock he felt on hearing the demand, but out of curiosity, he asked, 'How much is he asking for?'

'Twenty-five crore. Five crore has to be given in advance. The rest can be paid after receiving the appointment orders,' explained the middleman.

Suppressing the desire to laugh, Balagurusamy just said, 'I don't have that much money.'

'Sir, we know you very well; you are honest. You donated your salary to the Chief Minister's Fund when you were the vice-chancellor. I can arrange people who will provide you with it. They will take care of everything,' the man continued with confidence. 'The proposed post is for the Andaman and Nicobar Islands, which will be under the sole control of the lieutenant governor. The central government allots about 1500 crore every year for the administration of the Union Territory. It is the lieutenant governor who receives the amount. If 10 per cent of that amount is kept aside as commission, you will be able to make 750 crore in five years,' the man explained how Balagurusamy could make money as a lieutenant governor.

'There are so many people waiting for a chance to do all this. Why don't you approach them? Why have you chosen me?' Balagurusamy enquired.

He had an answer for that too. 'If you are appointed, no one will suspect the government of any illegal dealings; that is why they want you.'

'Is it not an illegal dealing? You better approach someone else for such matters. Do not come to me with such plans. How dare you make such a suggestion even after knowing how I hate such illegal dealings?' Balagurusamy demanded angrily before sending him out of the room.

Anger and wonder at what was happening in the country vexed him for a long time after that.

Novel Interviews

Balagurusamy proposed some new ideas which would help in learning how sincere the candidates for the civil services were towards the profession they wanted to enter and to encourage them.

He used to present them with cards containing 'life quotes' of famous people like Vivekananda, Mahatma Gandhi and Nelson Mandela. The candidate was asked to choose one of the cards randomly, read it aloud and explain its meaning, and show how that would be applicable and used in his or her work. This would bring out the candidate's analytical abilities and critical thinking skills.

Before the end of the interview, the candidate was also meant to ask two questions to the interview board members. Depending on the relevance and importance of the questions, the board could decide upon the candidate's general knowledge and his attitude and concern towards specific issues facing the nation. Asking right questions is more important than giving correct answers.

Before leaving the room, Balagurusamy would offer chocolates to the candidates and bid them farewell with a handshake and encouraging words.

BREAKING PRECEDENTS

Generally, the number of candidates invited for the interview for the civil services would be two and a half times the number of expected vacancies. It was the practice not to give more than 80 out of 100 marks for the interview. Once, Balagurusamy gave 83 marks to a candidate who had performed brilliantly. As a couple of members brought this to the notice of the chairman, he called Balagurusamy to enquire.

'As we have fixed 100 as the maximum marks, candidates can naturally aim for that. Not giving them more than eighty is only a precedent. Can it be considered wrong to give more than eighty?' Balagurusamy asked. The other members also agreed with his argument. After a lengthy discussion, the chairman also felt that the practice of not giving more than 80 per cent was not always justified.

On one occasion, Balagurusamy was supervising the main examinations to select candidates for the civil services being held at the Egmore Women's College in Chennai. The next day, one of the national newspapers published the news of his visit to the examination hall with a photo.

Seeing this, the chairman of the UPSC called Balagurusamy and said, 'The people should not know that we are conducting such an examination and supervising it. The UPSC has never done that.'

Balagurusamy, who always believed in transparency, was surprised to hear this bizarre argument.

'There is nothing secret about the UPSC conducting examinations, so there is nothing wrong with the report appearing in the newspapers. It is only through such reports that the people will learn about the civil services examinations and the work done by the UPSC,' said Balagurusamy.

Only a person of honesty, impeccable integrity and administrative ability can become a member of the UPSC. As he possessed each of these qualities in abundance, Balagurusamy was able to do justice to that position and perform his duties in an exemplary manner.

34

Painful Parting

*Existing yesterday, today to nothing hurled,
such (is the) greatness of this transitory world.**

—Thirukkural 336

Prof. Balagurusamy and Prof. Sushila were an epitome of companionship, theirs was a relationship described as 'made for each other'. Sushila was a very efficient teacher of management studies and was responsible for developing many new schemes that helped guide her students forward in the best possible manner.

In those days, personality development was a term no one had heard of. But Sushila had the foresight to see how important this was going to be seventeen years before it came to be widely used. Many could not do well in their profession even though they were qualified. The personality development scheme aimed to find such people and guide them to greater heights in their careers. Prof. Sushila named this 'Personality Re-Engineering'. Similarly, she developed another programme named 'Re-Engineering Teaching Skills' for bettering the teaching skills of college teachers. She gave special training under this program for teachers of more than a hundred colleges. Thus, Prof. Sushila gained as prominent a position as Balagurusamy in the field of education in Tamil Nadu.

Sushila also started a programme for the training of all employees (other than teachers) under Anna University. This got a very good response from all quarters of society. The programme envisaged developing a good, friendly relationship among the students, teachers and the non-teaching staff. She did this as a voluntary service, not

---

*This couplet has been sourced from www.ytamizh.com

taking any payment from the university. Sushila also managed the EBG Foundation, which was formed to further the efforts of development in the field of education. Many financially backward students have received aid from the Foundation.

Sushila never interfered in Balagurusamy's official work. She confined herself to her own field of activities and did much to use her abilities for the betterment of teachers and students. She envisaged many schemes aimed at empowering women and put them into practice. She was interested, like Balagurusamy, in encouraging those who were in the lower strata of society and giving them a helping hand to come up in life.

Balagurusamy wanted to return to Coimbatore after completing his term at the UPSC. But Sushila wished to remain in Delhi. While they were in Delhi, Balagurusamy and Sushila had visited President Pratibha Patil many times. These visits led to a friendship between Pratibha Patil and Sushila.

Members of the UPSC are not allowed to visit ministers or high-level officers of the government, but they can visit Rashtrapati Bhavan. That is because the UPSC is under the President of India. At this time, Sushila had developed a new programme entitled 'Healthy Living'. When Pratibha Patil came to know of the details of the scheme, she suggested that it could be implemented in states like Maharashtra and Gujarat. Sushila was also interested in it. So Sushila decided to remain in Delhi for work while Balagurusamy shifted to Coimbatore. She stayed in the three-bedroom Scottish Villa that Balagurusamy had bought for her in Gurgaon. Of the three cars they had, one was left in Delhi for Sushila, and the other two were sent to Coimbatore.

Compassion for All

Sushila followed the idea that Rabindranath Tagore had expressed in one of his poems: one should have compassion for all living things.

'Amma wouldn't allow anyone to call her pet dogs as "dog". They were "Number one" and "Number two" for her. She loved

them so much, and they reciprocated the same affection towards her,' said Bhagya, who had worked in Sushila's house for many years.

While they were staying in Coimbatore after Balagurusamy retired from the post of vice-chancellor, they had three dogs at home. When Balagurusamy went to Delhi to take up the post as a member of the UPSC, Sushila wanted to take the dogs with her to Delhi. So Sushila and Bhagya travelled in two cars with the three dogs for four days to reach Delhi.

'No other woman would show so much courage. It was surprising that Sushila was ready to take up the challenge with none other than the drivers to help her during the long journey,' said Balagurusamy once about that trip.

On reaching superannuation from the UPSC on 3 May 2010, Balagurusamy left Delhi for Coimbatore.

Balagurusamy and Sushila never compromised their individuality and independence. They often had to stay separately, as per the requirements of their responsibilities. Under the new circumstances, Sushila stayed at the villa in Gurgaon with a helper, Kala Devi. Two of the employees of the UPSC, Parameswaran and Vijaya, both from Tamil Nadu, were there to extend any help if Sushila needed it. Sushila did not use a cell phone and would talk to Balagurusamy on the landline.

On 4 July 2010, Balagurusamy got a message from Sushila's neighbour. 'Sir, Sushila Madam is not well. She is not coming out of the house. Her helper is not with her now.'

Balagurusamy was shocked to hear this. He left instructions to inform Parameswaran of the UPSC about it and started for Delhi by the first flight the next day.

Parameswaran and Vijaya were at the airport to receive Balagurusamy, and they came with him to the house. When he met her, Sushila was very weak. Kala, the woman who stayed with Sushila, had gone to Chennai to attend to some family matter. Balagurusamy wanted to employ somebody else for the duration, but Sushila had refused it. So he decided that he had to be in Delhi until Sushila regained her health.

He contacted his friend, Sundara Raman, who had been working in the British Council earlier, and made arrangements to have Kala sent to Delhi as early as possible. Once Kala returned, Vijaya also came to stay and help Sushila there. Slowly Sushila regained her health.

'What can I do for you, Sushila? I can't leave you in such a state,' lamented Balagurusamy.

Sushila revealed her desire to spend the rest of her life at the Brahmakumaris Ashram, a spiritual centre at Mount Abu in Rajasthan, and Balagurusamy agreed. But he wanted her to regain her health completely before she left. So he made arrangements for her treatment at the Columbus Hospital nearby. It was a well-equipped hospital with modern facilities. The doctors could not find anything serious with Sushila except for a deficiency of some minerals. The doctors wanted her to be in the hospital for two days, but Sushila insisted on going home. So she was taken home, and Kala was there to take care of her.

But that night, Sushila left this world forever.

Balagurusamy sat beside her, wracked with unbearable sorrow. He then informed their friends, colleagues, Sushila's brother and others about her demise. By morning, most of them were there. Her body was cremated at the electric crematorium near Lodhi Road at 12.30 p.m. on 7 July.

Sushila believed in religious rituals, and Balagurusamy, though an agnostic himself, made all arrangements to have her last rites performed by the priests. On 8 July, Balagurusamy immersed her ashes in the Ganga at Haridwar. Sushila, who joined him at a point in his life for a life together, had left him halfway through it. She remains forever in his heart. Very soon, Balagurusamy sold the house in Delhi and settled down in Coimbatore. Sorrows that deaden the soul can only hope for time to deliver solace.

35

Uncompromising Stand

The small the paths of ease pursue,
the great achieve things rare to do.

—Thirukkural 26

Balagurusamy is never ready to compromise when it comes to principles. When he came to Coimbatore from Delhi, many deemed universities invited him to be their advisor; others invited him to occupy very high positions. But he rejected all such offers without ever pausing to think. Some educational institutions wanted to honour him, but he declined such invitations also.

Balagurusamy got a letter from a newspaper group requesting him to preside over a discussion on education that they were organizing. He accepted the invitation. His name appeared on the invitation that he later received.

Upon going through the invitation, he realized that the meeting was to be conducted in a five-star hotel under the sponsorship of a deemed university. Balagurusamy had taken stringent actions against this very institution for irregularities in their work when it was only a college. So he was in a dilemma. He did not want to participate in a programme that this institution was sponsoring.

When the organizers met him, he spoke to them quite openly. 'You must excuse me. I will not take part in this meeting. This is being sponsored by a private educational institution. If I take part in it, it will mean that I morally support all that that institution is doing.'

The organizers suggested an alternative. 'Sir, you can keep away from the discussions. But please attend the programme. Many teachers and students are waiting to meet you. You can meet them individually and offer your guidance.'

'If I come there without participating in the discussions, it will only be like "visiting a bar to change your money". So please do not expect me to be present at this programme.'

Balagurusamy made his stance quite clear.

Another time, a new vice-chancellor of Anna University invited all former vice-chancellors to honour them. In the list of invitees, Balagurusamy noticed one man against whom he had taken legal action for corruption. Balagurusamy decided to keep away from that function because of this. He was not ready to change his stand even when he was told that Dr Abdul Kalam would be the chief guest for the function.

But all this must not be taken to mean that Balagurusamy is adamant. It only shows that he is not ready to do anything that goes against his principles. It is a well-known fact that if those who had to face legal action for their misdeeds repented and changed their ways, Balagurusamy was ready to accept them.

'What can you say of the habit of using your position of power to amass money rather than using it for the betterment of society?' said Balagurusamy, saddened by the prevailing trend among the educated. Whenever he was offered a high post, he saw it as a chance to serve society. He never acted against the dictates of his conscience, never misused his power or used his passion for personal gains.

Balagurusamy spent his free time participating in discussions on matters connected with education in schools and colleges. He was reluctant to participate in public meetings. He appeared on television usually for discussions based on issues related to education. He never kept any notes on the subject when he participated in any discussions.

SUPER KIDS

One day, in November 2011, when Jaya TV invited him to be a mentor for a programme on education, he refused to accept it. But when it was revealed that Chief Minister Jayalalithaa was particular about having him as the mentor, he agreed. It was a programme entitled 'Super Kids' based on general knowledge for schoolchildren. It would go on air for fifty-two weeks. Balagurusamy gave all the necessary guidelines to the producers to conduct the programme. It was hosted by Anu Hasan, niece of the actor Kamal Haasan. The producers invited Balagurusamy to the production studio when the shooting began.

'Sir, there will be a blue curtain in the background during the shooting. Many images, suitable for the occasion, will be made to appear on this curtain later on. As the background is blue, if you wear a blue shirt, it will lead to problems for the visuals. So please change the blue shirt,' the producers requested him.

'I always wear blue full-sleeved shirts. That is a part of my identity. So I cannot change it. You may use other colours for the curtain,' Balagurusamy replied.

In any case, episodes for ten weeks were shot and made ready. Due to some unknown reason, the programme was not telecast on Jaya TV. The rest of the episodes were not shot.

DEBATE ON THE NATIONAL EDUCATION POLICY

On another occasion, he had to participate in a discussion under the auspices of the People's Forum of a famous television channel in The topic of discussion was the New Education Policy (NEP) of the central government, with the participants sharing their views on whether the policy was 'affirmative or saffronised'.

'The NEP is a comprehensive, insightful document and it provides a detailed road map for achieving the educational goals and aspirations of twenty-first-century India. Ninety per cent of the new education policy is meant to achieve overall progress in the educational sector in the country. About 10 per cent of the recommendations need reconsideration and must be subjected to rethinking. The New Education Policy must be made 100 per cent perfect before implementation,' Balagurusamy said.

Balagurusamy's opinions and suggestions are always supported by facts and available documents. At times, he would also become emotional and passionate about the things he cared about; his sincerity would reflect in his words. He never shied away from pointing out the defects in the educational world. During the debate, he stressed that if India had not been able to achieve the required standard in education even after 75 years of independence, it was only because of the corruption that ruled that sector and unnecessary interference by politicians. He further felt that unless these two evils would be eradicated, it were almost impossible to achieve global standards in education.

He is always ready to offer suggestions for improving higher education in India.

WHY NEET?

At a channel discussion held by the same television channel at Erode, the topic of debate was whether the National Eligibility cum Entrance Test, popularly known as the NEET examinations, were necessary for students from Tamil Nadu.

'When students from all over the country, including the not-so-well-developed states like Bihar and Jharkhand, are ready to write the examination, why can't the students from Tamil Nadu do so? Such a stand would be shameful for a well-developed state like Tamil Nadu,' Balagurusamy strongly expressed his opinion.

He thought that the system of selecting candidates through NEET would go a long way in improving the standard of medical education in the country and eliminating the menace of capitation fees in admissions. Students could study in any state, and even outside India, once this system was in place.

RESERVATION FOR ECONOMICALLY WEAKER SECTIONS

'Should Reservations be Based on caste or Financial Capacity?' was the topic for discussion at another meeting conducted by the People's Forum at Nagercoil. Balagurusamy aptly explained the advantages and disadvantages of reservation.

'Reservation based on caste has been followed in the education and employment sectors for seventy years. Reservations, without any performance limits, have adversely affected the standard of education and the growth of the public sector. This has led to the deterioration of governance in all areas. We may have caste-based reservations with certain minimum qualifying performance criteria. Because of the available reservations based on caste in admission to higher education institutions, many students who have high marks fail to get admission. Many of them go abroad for their studies. This is a significant loss for the nation. A large segment of our population who are economically weak and live below the poverty line are not covered under any reservation schemes, and therefore, they do not receive any benefits. So I feel that reservation based on financial ability is an important step forward in ensuring social justice for the poor, and it should be introduced,' he opined.

It is heartening to see that his thoughts have been reflected in the central government's new reservation policy. All his opinions are well thought out and pronounced without leaving any room for doubt. Naturally, his words are thus taken seriously by those in power.

UNIQUENESS IN CHOOSING THE VC

One morning, when Balagurusamy was at his office in the Planning Commission, the secretary to the Governor of Tamil Nadu called him to say that the governor had appointed him as the chairman of the search committee for the selection of a suitable candidate for the post of the vice-chancellor of the Thiruvalluvar University in Tamil Nadu. The other members were Prof. S.P. Thyagarajan, former vice-chancellor of Madras University, and a retired professor from Madurai Kamaraj University.

Balagurusamy, while accepting the offer, said to the secretary that no recommendations would be entertained in selecting the candidate for vice-chancellor. He intended to identify the three most competent candidates who could lead the university with unbiased honesty and administrative acumen.

He wanted to learn about the opinion of the university's teaching staff on this matter. Therefore, after the committee had analysed the biodata of the candidates in detail, they went to the university and held discussions with the teachers and the other employees. Thus, for the first time in the history of Tamil Nadu, the selection of the vice-chancellor was held in a democratic manner.

Thiruvalluvar University had not been granted the 12B grade, like the other universities in the state. This grade would entitle the university to get financial aid from the central government. This fund could be utilized for the all-round development of the university. The teachers and the other university staff wanted to have a person who was capable of getting this status for the university to be appointed as the vice-chancellor. The new vice-chancellor should be one who was ready to speak his mind, be unbiased in his attitude and unwilling to bow before the pressure from those in power, they said.

The committee examined the candidates' educational qualifications, teaching experience, competency in conducting research projects, leadership qualities, the research papers published and the details of the national and international seminars in which they had participated.

The committee then shortlisted twenty candidates and requested them to submit their vision for the university, including their plan for the overall development of the university.

After considering all the inputs and detailed discussions, three names were arranged in alphabetical order, and the list was submitted to the governor. Prof. Gunasekharan was chosen as the new vice-chancellor. He was later able to get the 12B accreditation for the university, which was something the whole university was looking forward to.

'The selection of Gunasekharan showed Balagurusamy's ability to gauge the capabilities of a person through a psychological approach,' remarked Prof. S.P. Thyagarjan.

Balagurusamy was also the chairman of the committee appointed to select the vice-chancellor of Gandhigram University at Dindugal, a deemed university under the central government. Prof. Anandakrishnan, chairman of IIT Kanpur, and a vice-chancellor from Gujarat, were the other two members. Balagurusamy followed almost the same procedure here too. Some central ministers tried to intervene to give their recommendations for some candidates, but Balagurusamy did not entertain any recommendations. He stood firm on his principles.

36

Humane to The Core

*The wealth of a wide-hearted soul
is a herbal tree that healeth all.*

—Thirukkural 217

While Balagurusamy was working in Bangalore as the director of the Mahaveer Educational Institute, a husband and wife used to work in his house as domestic workers. Prof. Sushila had come to Bangalore a few days before the birthday of this couple's child. Balagurusamy and Sushila went to their house for the child's birthday. They felt sad upon seeing the condition of the house in which they were living. It was an old house, and the roof leaked when it rained.

Balagurusamy made arrangements for repairing the house the next day itself. That thatched house became a concrete building in a few days.

In the 1990s, when Balagurusamy was the director of the PSG Group of Educational Institutions, Bhagya was employed to work at his house. No one could beat Bhagya when it came to preparing delicious food. Both Balagurusamy and Sushila treated her with love, and she continues to work in Balagurusamy's house even today. Balagurusamy bought a two-portion house in Coimbatore for Bhagya, who came from a low-income family. Bhagya has given one portion on rent and gets additional income. Balagurusamy bore all the expenses for the ceremony when Bhagya's son got married.

When Sushila was staying alone in Delhi, Kala used to stay with her and work in the house. She looked after Sushila with great care when she fell ill. Kala, too, belonged to a low-income family, and Balagurusamy bought a house for her at Kovilambakkam in Chennai. He also made arrangements for Kala's daughter to pursue her profession as a beautician. He sent an amount of ₹5,000 for the education of Kala's grandchildren till they completed their education.

On 31 August 2021, Prof. Balagurusamy presented house plots to Bhagyalakshmy, Krishnaveni, Prabhavathi and Bhuvaneswaran, who are now working in his house.

Sheela, another woman who worked for him, was given land to build a house. He paid for the educational expenses of the son and daughter of Sumathy, who worked for him at Coimbatore. Ramalingam, who used to work as his driver, was given ₹5 lakh to build a house.

Once, the chairman of a private college came to see the vice-chancellor. He talked about various matters, making it apparent to Balagurusamy that the man had some hidden agenda behind the visit. Though he understood this, Balagurusamy gave him no chance to get to the point. The man had a packet in his hands. The vice-chancellor did not ask him what it held. After some time, the man got up to leave. At that moment, the phone rang, and Balagurusamy started talking on the phone. The man left, making use of the opportunity; he also left the packet on the chair. When Balagurusamy finished his conversation on the phone, he noticed the packet on the chair.

He immediately sent one of the staff to call the man back.

'You were trying to leave it here for me. Take it back. Don't try such tricks here,' he said and gave it back to him.

On another occasion, a man came to see Balagurusamy, making it seem that it was just a courtesy visit. He went on praising Balagurusamy to the skies. He referred to Balagurusamy's unique position among all the computer experts in the world. Balagurusamy felt almost suffocated as he heard all this when finally, the man came to the point. He wanted Balagurusamy to intervene and get admission for two people close to him.

'So, you went through all this talk for this, didn't you? Don't you know that I would never do such things?' Balagurusamy said and sent him out immediately.

Those with a PhD degree generally add 'Dr' before their names. Once, when he was travelling by train, his name was recorded as Dr Balagurusamy on the list of travellers. During the journey, one of the passengers fell sick. The authorities tried to find out if there were any doctors among the passengers. They saw the name, Dr Balagurusamy, and approached him to offer assistance to the sick man. He told them that he was not a medical doctor. As they continued to appeal to him, saying that the man was in a critical state, he had to open his suitcase to show that he did not carry the paraphernalia of a doctor—like a stethoscope or a blood pressure apparatus. When they saw the books in the suitcase, with the name Dr Balagurusamy ME, PhD printed on the cover, they realized their mistake. After this instance, Balagurusamy wrote 'Prof.' instead of 'Dr' before his name.

Once, on a visit to China, Balagurusamy went to a bookshop in Shanghai. He saw a book in Chinese with his name written in English on the cover. He showed the book to the saleswoman, and she told him the price. He was shocked to see how costly that book was. Out of pure curiosity, he asked her why that book cost so much.

'Why do you ask that? This author, Balagurusamy, is a great scholar. There is a lot of demand for this book in the Mandarin language. All the students who study computer science and engineering buy these books,' the woman said, giving him a sales pitch. Balgurusamy felt happy to see that his books were popular even in China. But he realized immediately that his book had been plagiarised into the Mandarin language. He informed his publisher, McGraw Hill, in Singapore about it. Then, McGraw Hill started publishing all his books in Mandarin too.

Once, an announcement appeared in the newspaper.

```
'The   pet   dog   of   Balagurusamy,   the   vice-
chancellor, is missing. Anyone who finds it will
be rewarded.'
```

Both Balagurusamy and his wife Sushila loved dogs. They looked after pets as if they were their own children. Both of them were depressed when their pet went missing from home. Sushila couldn't even eat properly. Many dogs were brought to Balagurusamy, and he understood the real purpose behind this. Though none of them was his, he paid some money to those who brought the dogs to show him. Then, he got the information that his dog was in a house at Saidapet. He went there immediately and got the dog back and gave him food and medical care. Later, he learned that the 'act of kidnapping' had been enacted by some people in the university with vested interests.

TSUNAMI IN TAMIL NADU

Apart from his work in the field of education, Balagurusamy involved himself in social service also. But it was never publicized. One day, early in the morning, he called Jayapalan, the controller of examinations, and Gopinath, the legal officer, and the three of them got ready to go to Nagapattinam by car. It was the day after the tsunami had lashed the coastal regions in December 2004. The chief secretary to the government was already there. They tried to comfort those who had been affected by the disaster. Balagurusamy handed over his contribution to the welfare fund for the tsunami victims to the collector. It was 11.15 a.m. when they went to see the victims who had been given shelter in a school, nearby. There, a girl stood up on seeing him and with folded hands, said, 'Sir, aren't you Balagurusamy, the vice-chancellor? I am a second-year student of Masters in Computer Application. We study your books.'

'Good. Are you all comfortable here? Are you getting enough food and water?' he asked her.

'We have not got any food till now,' she said, and soon others started talking to him. 'The children have not got any milk. When we asked for it, they said they would give us rice, and we should cook it for food,' said a woman, holding her crying child close.

Balagurusamy got angry and called the officer in charge of the camp and spoke gravely. 'How can these people cook in a temporary centre like this? Make arrangements for food for all the people and milk and biscuits for the children. I will wait here till all this reaches them.'

Balagurusamy left for Chennai only after ensuring that all those staying there had got what they needed. As soon as he reached Chennai, he contributed ₹1 lakh to the Chief Minister's Relief Fund.

There is none to equal Balagurusamy when it comes to following a simple life. Prof. Peer Muhamed, who was the director of affiliations at Anna University, said, 'He took us along with him to Tirunelveli for an inspection of one of the colleges. "I am taking you to a new place for dinner today," said Balagurusamy, and we naturally thought he must be taking us to a high-end restaurant. But he took us to a street food shop on the banks of the Thamirabharani River. Many people were having their meals there. He requested us to sit around a plastic table on the roadside. What we got from there was very delicious food, but it came as a surprise to us that a vice-chancellor ate from such a shop.'

TAMIL NADU STATE PLANNING COMMISSION

In 2011, when Jayalalithaa came back to power, she reconstituted the State Planning Commission of Tamil Nadu and she invited Balagurusamy to be a member. A retired IAS officer had already been appointed as the vice chairperson of the Planning Commission. Balagurusamy spoke to the chief minister, saying that it would be improper for him to take such a position when he had been in a position equivalent to that of the Judge of the Supreme Court.

'It will not be like that. You have to be concerned only with improving the standard of education in Tamil Nadu. You will have all the freedom to work on your own. You will not be under the retired IAS officer. I am the chairperson of the Planning Commission,' the chief minister made her intentions clear.

Balagurusamy decided to work as a member of the Planning Commission, but only under certain specific conditions. He had agreed because it was a request made by the chief minister personally and as it concerned the development of the educational structure in his state. One of his conditions was that he would neither stay in Chennai nor be a full-time member; instead, he would do it as part-time work. The other condition was that he would not accept any remuneration for the job.

However, he went to the office almost every day and worked earnestly and responsibly. He first conducted discussions with the heads of all the educational institutions in Tamil Nadu to appraise himself of the standard of education in the state. In all these discussions, he stressed the desire of the chief minister to make Tamil Nadu first among all the states in the matter of education. The discussions were to find out what had to be done to achieve that.

The Twelfth Five-Year Plan for the country was being implemented. Balagurusamy concentrated his attention on a higher standard of education and better opportunities for the younger people. To that end, he constituted a task force on Education. The members of the task force held detailed discussions on the place of education in the Twelfth Five-Year Plan. There were industrialists, government officers, prominent people from the world of sports, and experts from the field of education in the task force. Based on these discussions, they prepared a project report on the development to be achieved in education during the twelfth Five Year Plan. A new idea, named 'Balagursamy 6E Model', was introduced. The 6E Model comprised Expansion, Equity, Excellence, Employability, Eco-friendly and E-Governance. After submitting the report, Balagurusamy voluntarily resigned from the Planning Commission.

MARKS FOR MONEY SCAM

While he was on the Planning Board, Balgurusamy got a complaint about an irregularity in the process of re-evaluation at Anna University. The complaint was that one of the professors at Madras Institute of Technology (MIT) had given very high marks to students while re-evaluating their answer sheets. Balagurusamy went to MIT at Chromepet and wanted to meet the professor mentioned in the complaint. While he was in the office of the Dean of MIT, the Professor came and bowed respectfully before Balagurusamy and said, 'Sir, it was you who appointed me as a lecturer.'

'I am happy to hear that,' said Balagurusamy. 'Why don't we all sit down? I want to talk to you for a few minutes.'

The teacher was working in the computer science department. But he had corrected the papers in subjects with which he had no connection, like thermodynamics, mechanical engineering, and mathematics. First, the teacher denied doing anything like that, but he soon realized the seriousness of the issue.

'Do you think it is right to correct the papers on subjects that you don't teach and award more marks than what the students deserve?' asked Balagurusamy.

'What can I do, Sir? It is the vice-chancellor who made me do it. He gave me some registration numbers and instructed me to correct the marks and give 65 to 75 marks.' The teacher revealed his helplessness.

'Why did you not say no to such unethical practices?' quipped Balagurusamy.

'Sir, I won't be able to get my next promotion if I do not obey the vice-chancellor's orders,' replied the teacher.

Balagurusamy was astonished to hear those words and wondered how value systems in universities had deteriorated; teachers were willing to do anything for money and favours.

After noting down everything he had said, Balagurusamy said, 'You must write down all you said now.'

As the man hesitated, Balagurusamy said, 'If you do not give all this in writing, you will lose your job before five o'clock this evening.'

The teacher, terrified of losing his job, immediately wrote down everything and handed it over to Balagurusamy. The dean of MIT was not aware of any of these things. Balagurusamy did not waste any time handing it over to Governor K. Rosaiah. 'You are the chancellor of Anna University. If such things happen in the university, it will affect the image of the university and your reputation,' he reminded him. The governor was surprised to hear of such malpractices and promised to take appropriate action.

After waiting for a few days, Balagurusamy went to the governor's office to see what action had been taken on his complaint. He found that the governor had ordered that the complaint need not be considered. Balagurusamy then approached the minister for higher education.

'Don't bother about all that. They have only helped the students. Moreover, the government has no role in such matters,' said the minister. Balagurusamy was shocked to hear these words from a cabinet minister responsible for higher education.

A real fighter fights till the end when he learns that something is wrong. Balagurusamy would not close his eyes when corruption was taking place. He shared details of the whole incident with a national daily newspaper. This started a storm.

Chief Minister Jayalalithaa immediately ordered an internal enquiry to know more about the entire episode. It later became known as the 'Marks for Money' scam.

A committee was formed under the chairmanship of a senior professor to go into the allegations. As per the committee's recommendations, three teachers who had been involved in the incident were suspended. It was revealed that the teachers had acted according to the orders given by the vice-chancellor. As the vice-chancellor was involved in the entire process, the committee suggested that a high-level enquiry committee be set up for recommending suitable measures.

Strangely enough, no action was initiated even after the vice-chancellor left the post and joined back as a professor at the university. After keeping silent for an extended period, suddenly, to the surprise of everyone, he was suspended from service just a day before his retirement and a committee under the chairmanship of a retired judge of the high court was appointed to look into allegations against him.

After spending nearly a year in enquiries, the committee exonerated the former vice-chancellor from all the charges. Sometime later, the three teachers whom this man had directed to indulge in malpractices were dismissed from service. On hearing the news, Prof. Balagurusamy quipped, 'Where is justice? The arrows are punished while the one who aimed them is left free. It is a show of money power!'

BREAKING THE RED TAPE

Balagurusamy cared more about the achievements of others than his own. There were many occasions when he had to offer to give up his job to prevent the suffering of others. One such incident occurred when he was the vice-chancellor. Jayaraman, the registrar of the university, approached him one day.

'Sir, we have to issue a circular regarding the payment of salaries to the teachers and other officers of the university,' he said.

'What circular?' asked Balagurusamy.

'The salary of the university teachers and staff is generally deposited in their bank accounts on the first of every month. This time, we have not received the amount from the government. So we have to issue a circular stating that the salary may be delayed this month by more than a week or ten days,' explained the registrar.

Balagurusamy could not control his anger. 'A world-famous university! And it cannot pay the salary of the employees on time! What a shame! Do we have anything in the university fund?' he asked.

The registrar replied that there was not much left.

Balagurusamy contacted the education minister immediately on the phone, explained the situation and requested him to make the money available by the evening.

'Sir, I am not dealing with finance. I have to request the finance minister. Even if he agrees, the chief minister has to approve it, and then the cheque has to be sent by the finance secretary. All this cannot happen before this evening. So it will be better if you contact the Finance Minister directly and request him,' said the minister for education.

'How can I contact the finance minister? As the minister for education, you are responsible for all our matters. So you have to find a remedy for this. I have given my resignation letter to the Registrar. If the cheque is not received by this evening, you will get the letter tomorrow. I will no longer be in the chair of the vice-chancellor.' Balagurusamy thundered.

Balagurusamy immediately wrote his resignation letter, gave it to the registrar, Jayaraman, and said, 'If the money for the salary does not come from the government by this evening, hand over this letter to the government.'

Now the teachers and the staff were worried.

They all thought: How will the money come from the government today evening? It is impossible. Would Balagurusamy leave the university?

Some of them even made arrangements for a farewell to the vice-chancellor.

What happened next was nothing short of a miracle. An officer from the office of the chief secretary came to the office of the university with a cheque for ₹2 crore. Those in the office stood surprised at what had happened, Balagurusamy said to them, 'Nothing is impossible. If we work with conviction and determination, victory will be ours.'

Tri-Power

Alvin Toffler, a famous sociologist and futurist, in his book Power Shift has spoken about the trinity of power: knowledge, wealth and force. For Balagurusamy, his wealth came through knowledge, and the power that he derived was from his honesty. These are his strengths. His service is vital for the education field of the world.

MGR and EBG

There are some astonishing similarities between the former chief minister of Tamil Nadu, late M.G. Ramachandran, popularly called MGR, and E. Balagurusamy, known to his friends as EBG.

MGR has portrayed the characters that were assigned to him in the films with extraordinary acting acumen. EBG has exhibited his unlimited capability in all the work that was assigned to him in various fields. Most of MGR's characters were shown to be working towards the welfare of society, and they were all synonymous with humility. Whatever work EBG undertook, it would be characterized by his commitment to the upliftment of society and his humility. The characters portrayed by MGR are shown as trying to lead those who go astray on to the path of righteousness. If they did not change for the better, punishment was inevitable.

EBG, too, has been able to guide many private colleges that had committed irregularities, into the way of truthful functioning. And he has ensured severe punishment for those who were not ready to mend their ways.

MGR would never allow anyone who came to him for help go away empty-handed. Similarly, those who approach EBG for some help for a genuine cause can be assured of his unstinted support.

37

Abdul Kalam's Brother?

*Letter, number, art and science
of living kind both are the eyes.*

—Thirukkural 392

When Balagurusamy came to Anna University as the vice-chancellor, Dr Abdul Kalam was a professor emeritus there. He used to stay at the university guest house. The day after taking charge as the vice-chancellor, Balagurusamy had breakfast with Dr Abdul Kalam at the guest house. That was their first meeting.

'Balagurusamy, I know you well. I have read your book on reliability engineering. I have used the mathematical model in it in my research as well.'

Balagurusamy felt surprised and proud to hear these words from Dr Kalam.

Within a few weeks, the government under Prime Minister Vajpayee decided to elevate Dr Kalam to the highest office in the country as the President of India. The news of the election was received by 1 p.m. when he was with Prof. Balagurusamy in his office. He had to leave Anna University officially. Balagurusamy signed the paper permitting Dr Kalam to leave the post he was holding at the university.

Balagurusamy immediately arranged for a press meet and Dr Kalam addressed the media at 3 p.m. at the university guest house as the President-elect. Balagurusamy got the chance to witness the historic oath-taking ceremony of Dr Kalam as the President of India on 25 July 2002, at the Central Hall of Parliament, New Delhi.

Dr Kalam continued to keep in touch with Balagurusamy even when he was the President. Balagurusamy was a permanent invitee for all the functions held at Rashtrapati Bhavan. On certain occasions,

Dr Kalam would personally call him, 'Bala, you must come for this function,' he would say with affection.

Hairstyle

As a school student, Balagurusamy was a great admirer of Thiru. Karunanidhi, the impressive speaker and campaigner for the Dravida Munnetra Kazhagam (DMK) in the early 1960s. As admiration led to imitation, he started parting his hair in the centre like Karunanidhi. He keeps the same style, even today.

When he was the vice-chancellor of Anna University, he met the then chief minister of Tamil Nadu, Jayalalithaa, who was curious about this hairstyle. Without any hesitation, he revealed the truth that he was imitating the style of Karunanidhi.

The chief minister could only laugh as she heard it.

Something connects the two of them, even when it comes to the dates they were born: while Kalam was born on 15 October, Balagurusamy was born on 16 October. The date of birth given on the school certificate is different for some other reason. Since childhood, Abdul Kalam got all his support and help from his elder brother, Mohammed Muthu Meera Marikar, while for Balagurusamy, it was his elder brother Perumal who supported him. Both Abdul Kalam and Balagurusamy were born in humble families and rose through education. The word 'Kalam' means 'one who is proficient in speech'. Balagurusamy is another name for Lord Muruga, who is the samy who became the guru to his father, Lord Siva, while still a young boy.

Those who saw Dr Abdul Kalam and Balagurusamy together at Anna University campus used to say that they must be brothers. Dr Abdul Kalam became the President in 2002, and Balagurusamy became the vice-chancellor the same year. Everyone noticed their hairstyles, which made them stand out from the others. Abdul Kalam wore a blue full-sleeved shirt on most days. He would wear a coat only for the very special official meetings. Balagurusamy, too, always wore blue, full-sleeved shirts. He would wear a suit only for convocations, international seminars and the meetings where the chief minister was present. Both of them loved their students.

When Balagurusamy was in Hyderabad as the advisor to the Andhra Pradesh government, Abdul Kalam was also there as the director of the Defence Research and Development Organisation.

The ability to speak well is essential for a teacher. Both of them have proved that working constructively will ensure progress for the youth and the nation. Both of them are noted for their refined sense of humour and deep interest in Tamil literature. While he was the President, Abdul Kalam looked forward to any occasion to talk with students. He would enthusiastically respond to all their questions. Balagurusamy, too, had the same habit. He allowed students to visit him and submit complaints or suggestions. Like Abdul Kalam, Balagurusamy, too, follows a simple lifestyle. Anyone can visit him at his residence at any time. He loves to eat with others in restaurants. Both of them are well known for their honesty in public life. Both of them have completed their official tenures without a speck of blemish.

Abdul Kalam and Balagurusamy are famous as teachers who have followed their profession as a vocation. If Abdul Kalam was the 'People's President', Balagurusamy was the 'Students' Vice-Chancellor' at Anna University.

Though a Muslim, Abdul Kalam studied the Bhagavad Gita and the *Thirukkural* with reverence. The same is true of Balagurusamy. Though Prof. Balagurusamy is an agnostic, he believes in the essence of the Bhagavad Gita. When his first term in office was over, people thought that Abdul Kalam would be made the President of India for one more term. Similarly, many hoped that Balagurusamy would come back as the vice-chancellor for the second time. But those in power did not care to make use of the exemplary services rendered by each of them for a further period.

A TEACHER, A FIGHTER, A YOGI

Balagurusamy had started his career as a teacher, he continued as a professor and became a saintly figure. Like a river that flows along its own chosen path, with no thoughts of any personal gain, he continues with his work. The river's water can be used for drinking, irrigation of fields or for power production. Like the waters of the river, Balagurusamy, born into a rural agricultural family, started working on the farm, then he was a teacher, an advisor to the government, a vice-chancellor and a member of the UPSC. For him, all these positions were chances to serve the people.

Even today, he is as eager to know and learn new things as he has always been. Many colleges seek his advice and opinion. He uses these occasions to inculcate in the students the qualities of self-confidence, hard work and honesty.

He moves forward with the complete dedication of a born teacher. While holding an official position, he fights like a warrior who is not afraid of anything that goes against his sense of integrity. That courage to wage war for truth is still within him. When someone invites him for a function, he enquires about the aim of those who are organizing it and their history. If he finds them wanting in integrity, he uses those occasions to advise and correct them.

Balagurusamy continues to live like an ascetic, ignorant of the attractions of worldly possessions and pleasures. Swami Vivekananda and Thiruvalluvar are his heroes. He has put up their figures in the house that he has built. He often remarks that if there is one book that touches all the aspects of human life, it is the *Thirukkural*. On the pedestal of the statue of Thiruvalluvar in his residence are inscribed these lines:

> *The twain that lore of numbers and of letters give*
> *Are eyes, the wise declare, to all on earth that live.*[*]
>
> —Thirukkural 392

Balagurusamy has never chased wealth. It has come to him. He has never sought high positions. They have been conferred on him. The only thing Balagurusamy tries to amass is knowledge, and he is intent

---

[*]Thirukkural, *Thirukkural: English Translation and Commentary*, G.U Pope (trans.), CreateSpace Independent Publishing Platform, 31 August 2017.

on distributing whatever wisdom he has gained among others. He entertains the lofty aim of utilizing scientific knowledge for the benefit of the common man. As one who swears that his knowledge should be available to the Indian society, he refuses to accept lucrative positions abroad—making him a staunch patriot.

Balagurusamy's life is a living example, here to teach us that even for one born in difficult circumstances, the sky can be the limit. One just needs to be hard-working, honest and confident.

The facts of his life will continue to shine as a beacon of hope for the coming generations.

EBG: An Illustrious Life

POSITIONS HELD OVER THE YEARS

- Member, High Level Committee on School Education, Tamil Nadu
- Member, State Planning Commission, Tamil Nadu
- Member, Union Public Service Commission, New Delhi
- Chairman, Consortium for Educational Communications, New Delhi
- Vice-Chancellor, Anna University, Chennai
- Director, Mahaveer Academy Technology and Sciences, Bangalore
- Director, PSG Institute of Management, Coimbatore
- IT Advisor, Government of Andhra Pradesh

BOOKS

1. *Reliability Engineering*, Tata McGraw Hill, 1983
2. *Programming in BASIC*, Tata McGraw Hill, 1984
3. *Computers in Education& Training*, NIIT, 1984
4. *FORTRAN VI for Beginners*, Tata McGraw Hill, 1984
5. *COBOL Programming–A Self Study Text* Macmillan, 1989
6. *Artificial Intelligence in Industry and Government*, Macmillan, 1989
7. *Artificial Intelligence–Applications and Management*, McGraw-Hill, 1993
8. *Programming in ANSI C*, Tata McGraw Hill, 1990
9. *Expert Systems for Engineering and Management*, Ellis Horwood (UK), 1990
10. *Object Oriented Programming Using C++*, Tata McGraw Hill, 1995
11. *JAVA Programming–A Primer*, Tata McGraw Hill, 1998
12. *Numerical Methods*, McGraw Hill, 1999
13. *C and Data Structures*, McGraw Hill, 2001

14. *Programming in C#*, McGraw Hill, 2002
15. *Programming in ANSI C* (Mandarin Language), McGraw Hill Asia, 2006
16. *Object Oriented Programming with C##* (Spanish), McGraw Hill, 2007
17. *Fundamentals of Computers*, McGraw Hill, 2009
18. *Programming in ANSI C* (Korean Language), McGraw Hill, 2012
19. *Problem Solving Using Python*, McGraw Hill, 2016
20. *Python Programming* (Mandarin-Chinese Edition), McGraw Hill, 2017

AWARDS AND DISTINCTIONS

1. Chancellor's Best Graduate Student Award of the University of Roorkee, 1972-74
2. Mukhopadhyaya Medal for the Best PG Student of Electrical Department of the University of Roorkee
3. Gold Medal for obtaining highest marks in ME (Electrical Engineering), 1974
4. Khosla Research Award for the Best Research Work, 1974
5. Distinguished Leadership Award by the American Biographical Institute for his Contribution to the Computer Profession, 1988
6. Man of the Year 1992 Award by ABI, USA, for his outstanding accomplishments and service to society
7. Distinguished PSG TECH Alumni Award, 1994
8. World Lifetime Achievement Award by ABI, USA, for contribution in the area of Information Systems, 1994
9. Outstanding Fellow Award by the Institute of Engineers (India), 1996
10. Author of the Year 1998 Award by the Indian Council for Computer Education and Research
11. Rashtria Ekta Award by Global Economic Council, Karnataka, 1999
12. Bharat Nirman Excellence Award by Front for National Progress, New Delhi, 2000
13. Bharat Vikas Award, 2001
14. Seva Ratna Award by the Centenarian Trust, 2003

15. Vande Mataram Award during 27th International Conference on Oriental Heritage, 2004
16. DEED Award by Confederation of Indian Universities, New Delhi, 2004
17. Higher Education and Development Award by International Association of Education for World Peace, New Delhi, 2004
18. Lifetime Achievement Award by Indian Trade Promotion Organisation (ITPO), New Delhi, 2004
19. Nominated for World Technology Award in the field of Education, San Francisco, USA, 2004
20. Nominated for Padma Bhooshan Award by the Government of Tamil Nadu, 2004 and 2005
21. Dr Meghnad Saha Award by Indian Institute of Oriental Heritage, Kolkata, 2005
22. Sadhanai Thamizhar Award by Kolkata Thamizh Sangam, 2013
23. Lifetime Achievement, EMC Academy, USA, 2013
24. Listed in the Directory of International Who's Who of Intellectuals, UK
25. Listed in the International Directory of Distinguished Leadership, USA

Acknowledgements

This work would not have been possible but for the constant persuasion, encouragement and support of Dr Bindu Vijayakumar, Managing Trustee, EBG Foundation. We owe a deep sense of gratitude to her.

We would like to gratefully acknowledge the colleagues, friends and well-wishers of Dr E. Balagurusamy for providing us with invaluable insights and information during the preparation of the manuscript.

Our sincere and heartfelt thanks are also due to Sindhu K.B. and Hari Krishnan R. for their creative and constructive suggestions for improving the manuscript.

Finally, we would like to thank Dibakar Ghosh and his team for bringing out the book in its present form in record time.

③